future city
experiment and
utopia in architecture

future city
experiment and utopia in architecture

**Edited by Jane Alison, Marie-Ange Brayer,
Frédéric Migayrou and Neil Spiller**

Thames & Hudson

contents

Previous. Foreign Office Architects
Yokohama International Port Terminal
Yokohama, Japan 2002

foreword

Young British architects Chamberlain, Powell and Bon were first asked by the City of London to put forward designs for a bomb-razed Barbican site in 1954 – just prior to the moment that Constant Nieuwenhuys began to formulate his now-legendary *New Babylon*, a thrilling, utopian metropolis and the starting point of *Future City*. While the Barbican might be described as quintessentially British in its pragmatic approach to modernism, it would be easy to overlook the estate's own understated utopian ideals: the forward-looking commitment of its architects to the notion of the city centre, as opposed to the suburb, as a setting not just for work, but for thriving urban, cultural and social life. As such, Barbican Art Gallery provides a fascinating context for *Future City*.

This exhibition and publication would not have been possible without the collaboration of the FRAC Centre, Orléans and in particular the knowledge and enthusiasm of its director Marie-Ange Brayer. It has been a privilege to work with her. Marie-Ange Brayer, together with her predecessor in Orléans, Frédéric Migayrou, have shaped one of the most exceptional architectural collections in the world – unique for its comprehensiveness in the arena of experimental architecture, and for the unrivalled quality of its two- and three-dimensional works.

Future City has benefited from the generosity, support and expertise of a number of leading individuals and institutions in the field: Frédéric Migayrou, Chief Curator of Art and Design, Pompidou Centre; Jean-Marie Panazol, President, FRAC; Aaron Betsky, Director, Netherlands Architecture Institute; Max Risselada, University of Technology, Delft; Simon Smithson; and Donna Loveday, Design Museum, London.

Neil Spiller, with the support of Melissa Jones, has provided invaluable editorial support on this book, whilst also writing new introductory and biographical texts with great skill and speed. The exhibition has been enriched by the design of Foreign Office Architects. Their creativity and vision has led to an unusual synergy between the exhibition's form and content. We are immensely grateful for their respective contributions and for the cooperation of the many participating architects who have lent key works to the exhibition. Thank you to all of you.

Kate Bush
Barbican Centre

introduction

Jane Alison

'The only thing that is radical is space we don't know how to inhabit. This means space where we have to invent the ways to act and to live.'
Lebbeus Woods

Future City opens in 1956, the year that the Marxist, one-time CoBrA group artist, Constant Nieuwenhuys and the Parisian writer and provocateur, Guy Debord meet; the year in which Constant begins an architectural global utopia, New Babylon. Entirely speculative, Constant described it as 'another city for another life'.[1] It is with Debord and his band of revolutionaries drifting through the streets of Paris, calling for a new psychological understanding of the city and with Constant's vast network of zones made up of voids and buildings, constructions and deconstructions, that Future City takes its cue.

Yona Friedman's super-imposition of one city over another, Spatial City (1958–60), presents another critical starting point. Contemporary practices, such as OMA and MVRDV share Friedman's desire to maintain the existing city while allowing for a dramatic increase in population density. In looking at the urban situation, Friedman championed mobility over stasis, complexity over formalism. Above all, and unlike Constant, Friedman embraced the unpredictable and the chaotic growth of the urban situation in which the inhabitant is an active player.

The scene is set. Born out of a crisis in classical modernity, Constant and Friedman remain exemplars of what radical architecture can be. Debord's Situationism makes it impossible to conceive of architecture without people, movement or desire. For ten years and more, architects feverishly reinvented the city to be variously; spiritual (Székely), instant (Archigram), crater (Chanéac), floating (Kurokawa and Kikutake), compact (Pichler), oblique (Architecture Principe) and continuous (Archizoom and Superstudio).

Lebbeus Woods
(Detail) High Houses
Sarajevo, Bosnia and Herzegovina 1994–ongoing

Organic forms and processes inspired new ways of thinking about buildings and cities. New industrial materials sparked a proliferation of prefabricated capsules and pods for living and working. In this, Peter and Alison Smithson's sumptuous ergonomic House of the Future (1955–56) led the way. Early projects by Graham Stevens, Coop Himmelb(l)au and Haus-Rucker-Co further illustrate the '60s passion for alternative lifestyles, performance and inflatable forms. Archigram addressed popular culture and a new type of performative architecture is born. The playful interventions of this most British institution reverberate in the work of figures such as Will Alsop and Nigel Coates.

The verticality of Manhattan is replaced by the horizontal, a 'second urban order', in pioneering work of duo Claude Parent and Paul Virilio, who anticipated the folded forms and experimentation with surface that is prevalent today. Taking up where Friedman and Constant left off, architects such as Hans Hollein and Huth & Domenig imagined vast floated structures made up of capsules and 'plug-ins', so-called 'megastructures'. The Japanese Metabolists were hugely influential in taking the metaphor of growth and applying it to buildings and the city of the future. The Barbican itself is part of that same optimistic zeitgeist, some would say the last realised piece of utopian city planning in London.

In late 1960s Italy, Archizoom's No-Stop City (1969-72) and Superstudio's The Continuous Monument (1969) offered a merciless critique of society and architecture itself. In his final project at the Architectural Association, Exodus or the Voluntary Prisoners of Architecture (1972), Rem Koolhaas shows a clear debt to the radicalism of the aforementioned Italians. A pivotal figure within *Future City*, Koolhaas along with his OMA colleagues is represented by a further three projects produced over a thirty year period: original drawings for his celebration of urban congestion, Delirious New York (1976), a city within a building that is Jussieu Library (1992) and the iconic Beijing CCTV building, due for completion in 2008.

The revolutionary utopias and dystopias of the period 1956 to1976 period give way in the 1980s to the deconstructivist work of Tschumi, Eisenman, Libeskind and Morphosis among others. Grounded in theory and the ongoing scrutiny of architecture itself, deconstruction continues to renew itself. Since 1990 contemporary practice has been dominated by the revolution in digital technology. In practice this means architects have the capability to design ever more complex forms and to realise these with specialised computer driven tools, without ever having to fall back on standardized factory components. Folded, wrapped and undulating planes are characteristic of this new architectural domain. Computer generated data can be used to inform the very fabric of building and to re-think our future cities. Foreign Office Architects' Yokohama Port Terminal (1995–2002) is a marker in the intelligent utilization of data to create an outstanding public space, characterized by folded planes.

The boundaries between conceptual and installation based art and architecture continue to blur. *Future City* includes such influential figures as James Wines and Gordon Matta-Clark, but more recently studios such as R&Sie and Diller+Scofidio have each challenged our preconceptions of what architecture can and should be.

Future City maps an experimental lineage and charts architecture's fractured relationship to the city. It celebrates innovators and visionaries who have sought to extend the boundaries of their practice, those who have chosen to pursue the extraordinary over the commonplace. Yet *Future City* also raises important questions for the future of architecture and our cities. Yona Friedman predicted that by the year 2000 architecture would disappear, become invisible. And in the contemporary situation, especially in places such as China and Dubai, with iconic building the norm, architecture presents one seamless spectacle. When computer-aided design can lead to an obsession with formal complexity at the expense of an engagement with society, what constitutes the truly radical?

Lebbeus Woods makes work that responds to zones of crisis; places such as Sarajevo, Berlin, Havana. Out of sites of devastation he envisages new beginnings. He believes our future cities must be created from 'deep within the precise conditions existing in the present'.[2] Woods visionary forays into space are not intended to be realised but like so many of the works in *Future City*, this is beside the point. Architects must continue to reclaim the city, even if it is only on paper.

1. Constant Nieuwenhuys. IS no. 3, 1959. Quoted by Constant in an interview with Hans Ulrich Obrist, April 1999. Hans Ulrich Obrist Interviews. Volume I (Charta 2003).

2. Lebbeus Woods in Radical Reconstruction (Princeton Architectural Press, 1977) page 27.

the spirit of experimentation

Marie-Ange Brayer

Notions of utopia and experimentation in architecture have been the building blocks of the FRAC Centre collection. It encompasses projects that symbolize radical architecture from the 1960s to the very latest such work. Its extensive field of reference and its forward-looking dimension make it something of a treasure-trove of ideas about tomorrow's architecture, a place of open-ended reflection, which permanently questions and challenges architectural design procedures in ways that are both creative and critical. The FRAC Centre collection includes works by artists working in liaison with architecture and architects' projects; hence, emphasis has, from its earliest days, always been placed on the common aesthetic field likely to be shared by artists and architects.

The beginnings of the collection were formed in 1991, at the instigation of Frédéric Migayrou, the then new visual arts adviser at the DRAC Centre – the Orléans-based Regional Cultural Affairs Department – and currently chief curator of architecture and design (MNAM–CCI) at the Pompidou Centre in Paris. The aim, then as now, was not to put together a record of contemporary architecture, like some inert warehouse, or to draw up a soulless inventory thereof, but rather to develop an interest in architecture as experiment, utopia and research. Utopia here does not mean a denial of reality. On the contrary, in the implicit crisis besetting the rational order, it offers a critical glimpse of creative work and its sometimes visionary dimension. Michel Ragon, who defended this 'forward-looking' architecture in France in the 1960s, wrote in this regard: 'Unlike utopias of the past, present ones are almost all immediately achievable.'

Haus-Rucker-Co
Pneumacosmic Formation
1971

In its early days, around 1991–92, the collection turned its focus on 'deconstruction', which gained acceptance in 1988 at New York's MoMA and duly acquired outstanding international projects. Gravitating around the French philosopher Jacques Derrida, American and European architects, among them Frank O. Gehry, Rem Koolhaas, Peter Eisenman, Zaha Hadid, Bernard Tschumi and Daniel Libeskind, stressed theoretical work and the conceptual dimension of the project. Thus, for Peter Eisenman, it was more pressing to 'conceive' architecture than to execute it. In this respect, Eisenman's Guardiola House (1986–88) presented the challenge of a 'textual' architecture, which borrowed from both linguistics and psychoanalysis. In 1982, the Coop Himmelb(l)au Open House project separated architecture from any kind of plan, on the grounds that the former was generated by the unconscious: a drawing made blindfold, like some form of automatic writing, would be the 'psychogram' of the project – its raw material – from which the other stages would emerge. The Open House has been reproduced in countless publications and has become the project that best symbolizes deconstruction. In 1983, Bernard Tschumi built the Parc de la Villette in Paris, the first city park to accommodate a variety of programmes, both formal and functional. Rather as in Derrida's writings, Tschumi here applied dissemination, contamination and disjunction, and resorted to film-editing techniques to develop a heterogeneous urban scenario; architecture as event. Berlin City Edge (1987) by Daniel Libeskind, whose most recent projects include the Jewish Museum in Berlin and the planned new World Trade Center in New York City, is one of this architect's most important experimental projects. By increasing the number of references, it is presented like an urban palimpsest that is decipherable in its complex, sediment-like layers. The 'architectural text', to borrow Libeskind's words, encompasses all texts and all cultures in their diversity and universality. The FRAC Centre collection also includes important projects issuing from Californian deconstruction – mainly individual houses (Michele Saee, Morphosis, Eric Owen Moss).

The FRAC Centre collection has also turned its gaze on the experimental architecture of the 1950s and 1960s in France. To this end, it has acquired Ionel Schein's earliest plastic architecture projects and dwelling sculptures by André Bloc, advocate in France of artistic synthesis, as well as editor of the magazine L'Architecture d'aujourd'hui. Quintessential projects from those years, which have hitherto received little attention, have also been included in the collection. We thus find a remarkable group of maquettes and drawings that illustrate the "oblique function" of Claude Parent and Paul Virilio. Together, this groundbreaking duo championed a topological approach to architecture, based on the notion of 'surface', something that is nowadays being explored by all architects with access to digital tools. The FRAC Centre collection thus proceeds by way of historical 'rebounds' and 'comebacks', in addition to rehabilitations of architects, today reinstated in the 'heritage' of contemporary architecture. We have only to think of the antecedence of Schein's plastic cells, produced in 1956, the first mobile autonomous housing units, well ahead of the projects of the Metabolists, and Archigram in England in the early 1960s. 'One of the factors justifying any collection is the world of comparisons that it suggests,' writes Christian Girard about the FRAC Centre collection.

The issue of mobility and of an architecture without ties is one utopia that is a common theme throughout the FRAC Centre collection, from Yona Friedman's Villes Spatiales to inflatable architecture. From the early 1960s on, Pascal Häusermann and Chanéac developed an architecture that was at once organic and modular, made up of conglomerations of cells. 'Architecture for everyone' was the creed espoused by Ionel Schein, for whom the prefabrication of parts and industrialization would enable everyone to have access to a dwelling or habitat, mass-produced and at the same time adapted to modern living. The collection's line of development consisted in making a synchronic cross-section in Europe, at a given moment in architectural research, bringing together, in one and the same collection, what might well be regarded as the last avant-gardes, the final encounter between art and architecture.

Major projects by Archigram (Peter Cook's and Ron Herron's Instant City; David Greene's Living Pod) were thus acquired, as were projects produced by radical Austrian architecture (Coop Himmelb(l)au's Villa Rosa; Haus-Rucker-Co's Pneumacosm; Walter Pichler's La Ville compacte; Eilfried Huth and Günther Domenig's Ragnitz, Medium Total and Floraskin). The megastructures, such as Huth Domenig's Ragnitz, that appeared at the end of the 1960s were no longer updates of Gropius's 'total architecture' but were defined by their capacity for extension and proliferation, by their transformability. Architecture was no longer an object, but an environment, a spatial field. Italian radical architecture is likewise splendidly represented in the FRAC Centre collection, from Superstudio's Histograms of Architecture to Archizoom's Letti di Sogno (Dream Beds) and Gianni Pettena's Ice House. The modern avant-gardes did share a common creed, but radical architecture no longer focused solely on irony, provocation and syllogisms. What counted was no longer the object but the situation and behaviour. Systems of productive logic for architecture were mixed together; new forms of 'localism' emerged in creative work.

The transversal evolution of the collection has led it towards projects that are nothing less than icons of contemporary architecture, resulting from the varied range of their interpretations. So the FRAC Centre owns, among other things, two major works from Rem Koolhaas's Delirious New York: In Flagrante Delicto and The City of the Captive Globe. These drawings are narrative forays into the 'urban congestion' of Manhattan, into the mechanistic subconscious of the City, which, for Koolhaas, is represented by the grid, a fantastic projection of all his experiments to come. In its collections, the FRAC Centre also has one of the most widely published projects in the world: Indeterminate Façade, by James Wines/SITE, built in Houston, Texas, in 1975. This commercial building, with its brick façade, which seems to be collapsing in the urban space, suspended between construction and demolition, raises the issue of context, and for the first time in architecture introduces the idea of indecision and uncertainty. James Wines would refer to this building as an 'assisted readymade'. This critical relationship to the identity of architecture is probably what encompasses the entire FRAC Centre collection, from Rem Koolhaas's Delirious New York to Daniel Libeskind's Berlin City Edge.

Today, having issued invitations over the past four years to some 150 different teams of up-and-coming architects to attend the ArchiLab conferences, initiated and produced by the City of Orléans, the FRAC Centre is continuing to support creative architectural work, exhibiting and backing young architects, French and foreign alike. In its own way, ArchiLab aims is to set up a platform of contacts among a generation of research architects from all over the planet. And today's 'research' architect probably stands somewhere between the quest for creative specialness and the need for a network of words and exchanges, between the responsibility of the concept and the acceptance of the complexity of reality (social, economic, anthropological).

Needless to say, the days of banners, flags and manifestos are over now; there is no longer any emancipatory task for architecture; there is no universal theory, no ideology to revere, no novelty to promote. In his Condition postmoderne, Jean-François Lyotard had already announced the end of 'grand narratives'. The doubts expressed by the architectural avant-gardes of the 1960s about functionalism and technology have given rise to today's new form of architectural operativeness, with a uniform levelling of procedures, systems of logic and projects. From Rem Koolhaas's 'dirty realism' to digital architecture, it is perhaps a new form of transitiveness that is being introduced, in its approach to reality that is both local and global: an architecture with 'differential intensities', which implode systems and formal arguments, ushering in a permanent questioning of the architect's praxis.

Instead of acquiring isolated 'objects', the FRAC Centre endeavours to present a project in its entirety, from the earliest sketches to the final maquette, so as to retrace the different phases of its formulation and work through the architect's design process. It is thanks to the unfailing support of the AFAA that the FRAC Centre has managed to show its collections throughout the world over the past few years.

Architecture is not only what is built; it is also a conceptual trajectory, the comparison of concepts stemming from heterogeneous disciplinary fields, which exempt it from all formal unification and open it up to its future development. This ceaseless exploration, which pushes architecture out to its conceptual and disciplinary boundaries, permeates all the projects in this collection.

non-standard orders:
'nsa codes'

Frédéric Migayrou

Non-standard. Can one specify or define non-standard architecture? The term 'non-standard' has meaning in two fields of knowledge, both of which upon first inspection appear totally heterogeneous. In its very formulation, the idea of 'non-standard' obviously evokes, on the one hand, a refusal of normalization, of widespread standardization as a fundamental factor of industrialization, as a determining principle of Modernism in that it endeavours to deploy standardized mass production. Beyond architecture, this trend has given birth to a one-sided world culture of production and products. But 'non-standard' also refers to mathematics, more specifically to 'non-standard analysis', the title of Abraham Robinson's 1961 publication.[1] Robinson conceived and laid out the theoretical foundations of this new branch of mathematics dealing with the development of infinitesimal calculus. Indeed, according to Robinson, infinitesimal figures can be assimilated into usable numbers in all operations of logic and fundamental mathematics. Robinson completes the hypothesis sketched out by G.W. Leibniz, who thought that the opposition finite/infinite was not absolute but relative. Non-standard analysis opposes the formalism of mathematical language, focused on its own objectivity, by introducing open, infinitesimal models, genuine tools of approximation that presuppose the nature of an external, constructive mathematical reality.[2] Beyond a mere debate between mathematical formalism and intuitionism, non-standard analysis posits a dynamic structuralism, an abstract semantics that underpins the interrelation between phenomena and meaning. It is the establishment of a general and formal hermeneutics that can become directly involved at the core of

EZCT Architecture & Design Research
Studies on Optimization: Computational Chair Design using
Genetic Algorithms (with Hatem Hamda and Marc Schoenauer)
2004

an overall physics of phenomena. If this domain of mathematical analysis found immediate applications in so many disciplines – physics, biology, economics and of course in the field of computing – it was because this 'theory of models' goes well beyond the formal logic of the Vienna Circle to induce an implemented physics of meaning. René Thom, founder of this structuralism with morphogenesis, an a priori formalization of mutations in matter, spoke of a 'semiophysics'. Inferring the idea of a morphogenetic continuity in abstracto revolutionizes the very condition of the appearance of singularities, of the definition of form and of its meaning. Thus, reductionist theories, in which phenomena are restricted to descriptive systems, as well as phenomenology, which would remain at a descriptive distance, were brushed aside. The mathematical modelling of morphogenesis proposed by René Thom does not offer a description of general principles of physics, but the establishment of a differential model, a priori intended to bring to light the singularities in a process.[3]

In taking stock of contemporary architectural research, one is forced to acknowledge that the development of digital design applications has resulted in the widespread idea of a style, a type of rendering in which sequencing and kinetics have fostered the rise of a topological understanding. The vulgate of a geometry that is both critical of projective geometry as well as its Euclidean origins, carried forward by algorithmic systems, has developed into so many formalized themes, super-surfaces, hyper-surfaces, attempting to seize a topological vocabulary: folds, loops, nodes, layers ... Architectural design and the capacity for 'generative modelling' – a genuine, real-time, analytical tool that allows the form and the organization of the architectural programme seemingly to spring from a mere choice made from among a broad selection of other possibilities – may have become indissociable. What is more, the self-organization of these generative forms has widely developed into an organic understanding in which biological structures seem to embody new unities, a differential state of the architectural object. Comprehension of what non-standard architecture can be hinges on the specification of this change in status, of this identifying and component principle of architectural unity. Behind the flurry of publications, colloquia and the multiplication of exhibitions, all striving mainly to tackle the issues of representation or projection posed by the virtual nature of this digital space and by the generalization of a zone where cyberspace fosters an ultimate/new metaphysics of space, the tectonic shift in the founding order, in what can be the constituent logic of a new architectural singularity, seems to go unnoticed. Conversely, the hasty assertion of the advent of a 'virtual' architecture bears its own contradiction within itself.

Morphogenesis, topologies: the architecture to come is the object of widespread suspicion. It is tirelessly denounced as formalist in that, precisely because it reveals itself as a generator of infinite forms, it resists by its very essence any decree from an external order. The paradoxical tension between digital architecture, which carries with it the aura of dematerialization and the return of hylomorphism, in which the same models for matter could define the models of a built architecture, remains unresolved, if one insists solely on a critical questioning of form. By relying on fractal theories or those of morphogenesis, which pepper numerous articles of architectural criticism, thinkers are seeking to define how a singularity organizes itself within a dynamic system. Just like D'Arcy Thompson's biomorphic models, 'catastrophe theory' is seemingly exploited to elaborate a meta-geometry of matter founded on the idea of genetic mutation. Though the fields of biology and, closer to architecture, geography[4] already rely heavily on these types of modelling, for architecture they remain frozen in a descriptive approach, always assuming an external phenomenon that must be placed into a logical framework of comprehension.

For non-standard architecture this is precisely the issue, i.e. to go beyond the bounds of any assumptions about form, any anteriority or exteriority of a determining principle, of the elaboration of form. Architecture must therefore live up to its intrinsic capacity to specify, to bring singular elements to light. It must forcefully challenge an architectural tradition that has historically decided its language and syntax for the representation of an external normative principle, of a rigid restriction to orders, by counting solely upon its own structural capacities. This issue of canon, a question going back to the essence of architecture, underpins and goes beyond all relation to form. The definition of orders, of a plan in perspective, which organizes the principles of construction through the use of measure and proportion, architecture has always been nurtured by questioning its foundation: the fiction of classicism on the evocation of a forgotten origin, the earliest architecture of Marc-Antoine Laugier, the rational normative principles of J.N.L. Durand, though the elucidation of the conditions of this legal establishment has remained elusive. Even the transition from the classical field's codifying to the institution of industrial norms, to the genuine legal status conferred upon standardization, was no longer subjected to the question *quid juris*, as if the modulation of standards caught up in the flow of industrial production did not impose a rupture, another idea of architectural identity. It is in these terms that the philosopher Gilles Deleuze, in reference to an earlier text by Bernard Cache, 'L'Ameublement du territoire',[5] defines the domain for practising a properly non-standard architecture: 'It is a very modern notion of the technological object: it does not even refer back to the first wave of industrialization when the idea of a standard still retained a semblance of essence and imposed a law of constancy ('the object produced by and for the masses'), but refers rather to our current situation when the fluctuation of the norm replaces the permanence of the law, when the object positions itself in a continuum through variation, when automated digital production or the digitally operated machine replaces die stamping. The object's new status is no longer compared to a spatial mould, i.e. a relationship of form/matter, but rather to a temporal modulation that involves being continuously placed in a variation of matter as much as in a continuous development of form.'[6] Thus, Deleuze confers a legal as much as an ontological dimension upon this new standard of variability, echoing an ambivalence in the works of Leibniz vis-à-vis the foundation of Modernism within the baroque, which within the logic of the baroque distinguishes a structural field, the one with the monads defining the figures and the qualities, from the chaotic world of flows. To the distance maintained by the rational subject with regard to the object – a distance that conditioned all geometric relations of the system of perspective at the beginning, notably of the organization and ordering of the field of architecture – is opposed a correlation between the subject and the object where the point of view is maintained by the variation. The object exists only in the variation of its profiles and refers to a transformation that is a component of the subject. This is precisely the dynamic that Gilles Deleuze refers to as 'objectile'.

The 'objectile' assumes that the 'point of view' is caught up in the movement of variation, carried by continuous inflection and, as such, is a component of the subject. Perspective is interconnected with this following of modulation. The point of view is no longer defined by determining a distance, but rather through the range of all possible determinations. If, according to Deleuze, the 'objectile' merges with the 'geometric', this is because inflection imposes itself as the primordial genetic element, a perpetually cursive point that generates intrinsic singularities, resisting the establishment of pure and exact figures. The repeated mention of the active line, as Paul Klee called it, this 'non-dimensional point', 'between the dimensions', always refers to the ordering of the entire world, the cosmos, which the artist opposes to the indeterminacy of chaos. A line is ordered because it is carried by inflection; for Klee (*Formation of the Black Point*, 1925), as for Wassily Kandinsky (*Drawing for Point Line Plane*, 1926), inflection is most often expressed by drawing arrows indicating the component of tension, according to the idea of 'material-force', to use

Deleuze's term, returning to its baroque essence. This 'perspectivism' without distance, this relativism that is not a variation of the truth or of the normative principle according to the subject, whose source Deleuze finds in Leibniz, Friedrich Nietzsche or Alfred North Whitehead,[7] echoes an understanding of the baroque that remains largely hidden by classicism. The same is true for the serpentine, which for William Hogarth (*The Analysis of Beauty*, 1753) organized the codification of the body's movements in dance as well as in drawing or coming more directly from the differential geometry of Girard Desargues (*Rough Draft for Invasion of Privacy of the Events concerning the Encounters of a Cone with a Plane*, 1639), from the order that allowed arabesques in the gardens of André Le Nôtre or the anamorphic perspectives of Jean-François Niceron (*La Perspective curieuse*, 1651) . This infinite line of inflection, which Deleuze designates as a fold, is a virtual quality that differentiates itself unceasingly to self-actualize in a conscious event, a 'subjectile', or to realize itself in matter as an 'objectile'. Inflection is the indissociable composition of these two vectors, and intrinsically defines the principle of a legal mooring perpetually renewed, of a codification that does not reveal itself, which is beyond all representation of the law, a 'differentiation' of the norm. Bernard Cache, in a chapter of his essay entitled 'Subjectiles and Objectiles: Towards a Non-standard Mode of Production', takes up the issue of the generalization of parametric functions in the software applications managing machining, which make it possible to manufacture one-of-a-kind objects industrially, each one of the same series having a different shape, and questions this historic evolution of architectural order as it transits from codification to standardization. Although the rise of the standardized object did lead to the idea of variability, this notion remained limited to a repetition of type, a mismatch between the real aesthetic determination of variation circumscribed by the avant-gardes and industrial production limited by the Taylorism of the series. This norm, always in the process of being defined and always deferred, is transcribed into 'objects fluctuating on the variable curves of new industrial series ... There are no longer pre-established functions requiring a form; we have only the occasional functions of fluctuating forms.'[8]

However, one cannot so easily confront standard with non-standard in an antinomian mode, as if the ensuing deregulation established the new terrain of free expression. It is less a question of a normative system for Modernism than reconsidering its critical and aesthetic sources, ill served by a one-sided reading that believed it was moving beyond the modern moment by denouncing its formalism and its abstraction. The perpetual contradiction between the requirements of the industrial series and the preservation of architectural diversity, which form the basis of the earliest discourses on Modernism by John Ruskin or William Morris and which seemed fulfilled with the Bauhaus, was never interpreted in terms other than those of production, of an insoluble contradiction between the commercial constraint of repeating the same object the greatest possible number of times and that of industrially manufacturing different objects. This tension, which to this day animates the play between market forces and fashion trends, masks the critical return to the notion of the standard, the *Typisierung*, a questioning of the genesis, the identifying status of the 'type', of the idealization of the norm in an ultimate codification determined by use, raising the *Bauentwurfslehre* (Elements of Construction Projects; 1936) by Ernst Neufert to the rank of a legal manual. Yet, it is indeed the very idea of a singularity defined by the order of its qualifications that leads to Henry Van de Velde's earliest thoughts, to his struggling in the essay 'Die Linie'[9] to define the new industrial style. The line is not a decorative element, a hasty reading of the *Jungendstil* might conclude, but is indeed a 'dynamographic' system: 'A line is a force that functions in a way similar to all elementary forces: if a number of contradictory lines are assembled, they will exert effects similar to those produced by the interaction of elementary contradictory forces. When I say that a line is a force, for me, this is an observation of fact; the line derives its energy from the person who traces it. In this way, nothing is lost of the energy or the force.' Here, the line is invested with an anthropomorphic quality, inscribing itself like a metaphor of the inflexion and energy of the body in movement, thus echoing the Nietzschean body described in *The Will to Power* as 'a differential of qualified force'.[10] This line, which condenses both the body's energy and the dynamic of cognition, springs forth in arabesques in the *Danse serpentine* of Loïe Fuller (1902), but obviously rendered more technical, swept up in the sequential process of the machine by Etienne-Jules Marey. The body is transfigured into a cinematic object, going forth reciprocally by optimizing the dynamic: a diagrammatic line endowed with a prescriptive function, like the apparatus of Lillian and Frank W. Gilbreth, allowing for a rationalization of the body's movements at work or those of a housewife in her kitchen tending to her domestic chores. The Taylorism of the Gilbreths does not assert a simple mechanization of the body; it is, to use the words of Siegfried Giedion, 'the intervention of the machine in the very substance of both the organic and inorganic'.[11] It is in fact Siegfried Giedion who, seeking to understand the new space/time assumed by mechanization and, reflecting on the interchangeable nature of the elements that enable standardization, compares the 'pure form' of the movement engendered by mechanization to the experiments of artists in their quest for a spiritual and conceptual space, an enhanced space that could go beyond the geometric field. He shows, in a few well-known pages, the same concern that animated Bergson's lecture at the Collège de France in 1900, 'Le Mécanisme cinématographique de la pensée', and the work of the Gilbreths, Etienne-Jules Marey or Muybridge, and by referring to the *Nu descendant un escalier* by Marcel Duchamp as well as the inflected lines of Paul Klee or Wassily Kandinsky.

The entire understanding of the field of Modernism hinges on this problem of assimilating the new legal order flowing from this generic capacity for inflexion. This limitation of criticism is analysed by Detlef Mertins when he compares the still neo-Kantean aesthetic positioning of Siegfried Giedion with that of Emil Kaufmann. Whereas in *Space, Time & Architecture* (1941), Giedion unceasingly emphasizes the component of ambiguity in a mutual mediation of the subject and the object, where space is determined in a dialogue with the subject – pursuing the theories on *Raumgestaltung* initiated by August Schmarzow and then taken up by Theo Van Doesburg and László Moholy-Nagy – he remains enclosed in a neo-Kantean framework: 'The failure of the historical theories of Giedion and Kaufmann are symptomatic: the Modernist quest for a new normativity goes beyond the Kantean spirit without relying on the metaphysics of movement and differential that stirred the heart of all of Modernism's polemics.'[12] Then the crisis of the 'free line' occurred, following the exhibition 'Line and Form' ('Linie und Form') held at Krefeld by Henry Van de Velde, first founder of a school of applied arts in Weimar and whose mission was precisely to initiate new relationships between art and industry, i.e. a new logic for design. During this exhibition, which presented the photographs of a military boat, the critics, reacting in a climate of nationalism, seized upon the Yachting Style, on this call for fluidity. Along with the foundation of the Werkbund in 1907, the debate over relations between architecture and the world of industrial production became more radical, through a *sachlich* approach to design with clearly asserted production. The issue of the *Typisierung* involved two individuals in a virulent polemic: Henry Van de Velde and Hermann Muthesius, the first considering the standard as a dead and abstract system of norms, and the other asserting the type as the domain of shared conventions. The two parties born of this scission, one comprising Van de Velde, Bruno Taut and August Endell and the other including Hermann Muthesius, Peter Behrens and Walter Gropius, reflect this ambivalence attached to the standard, which was to leave its mark on all the architecture of the 20th century. The back-and-forth confrontation between the two groups fostered the legal mutation of the very idea of 'conception', the fact that the formation, the 'in-formation' of the object, or the *Gestaltung*, to use the word that anticipates the contemporary definition of 'design', is established as the conceptual approach directly articulated on the tools of production. For the evocation of a new style, still defended in 1902 by Hermann Muthesius in his famous work *Stilarchitektur und Baukunst*,[13] is substituted the assertion of an objective art (*sachlich*), freed from its last expressionist manifestations. 'Behind the apparent opposition separating Van de Velde and Muthesius, it is the internal duality of their conception of *Gestaltung* that prevails, seeking to reconcile and preserve a dynamic of creation at the heart of the new industrial aesthetic. Through the notion of *Typisierung*[14] one seeks this difficult reconciliation.'

Though the term *Gestaltung* became popular from 1903 onward, it was nevertheless overly determined by geometric 'normativity', which defines at once an abstract structuring of experience, space and material forms organizing space, structuring where the experience is connected to the internal requirements of materials and function. This new normativity, which dealt with the design of the house, furnishings and the applied arts, was achieved by 1919 with the publication of the review *Die Form*, by Walter Riezler, and thereafter with the exhibition 'Die Form ohne Ornament', which attempted to bring to light types and constants of industrial production. It is of course no longer a question of discrediting ornament, as Adolf Loos advocated (*Ornament und Verbrechen*, 1908), but rather of limiting the spiritual field of the mechanical era. Walter Gropius, in the Arbeitsrat für Kunst anticipating the Bauhaus project, calls for a genuine constructivist programme: 'We have all become builders whose purpose is to edify a cathedral of the future that will unify under a single Gestalt architecture, sculpture and painting.[15] Against all formalist interpretations of Modernity, the review G[16] – G for *Gestaltung* – will remain the authentic manifesto in the legal establishment of this new differential singularity, this abstraction carried forward by its physical achievement, to borrow from the phenomenological notion of *Einfühlung* of Wilhelm Worringer. In a remarkable analysis of the development of the concept of *Gestaltung*, Detlef Mertins indicates it is a process, the attempt to become form, to the becoming-form's linking without distinction to the spiritual domain, organic life or artistic and industrial productions. 'This orientation inherited from vitalism, shared by all the key contributors, was formalized in the most empathetic and esoteric terms by Raoul Hausmann. He suggested that each form was a frozen moment-image participating in the creative aura of the atmosphere (*fluidum*), a component idea for Hugo Häring, Mies van der Rohe and Le Corbusier as well, that had to contain the entirety of the normative immobility of the type and an opening to vitalism.'[17] The exigencies of a concrete, objective art, the search for a *Neue Sachlichkeit*, led the architects to resolve the antithesis between an abstract space, a space of mastery of geometric and even mathematical conception and a spatiality given over to the equally important dynamic component of the body. Pursuing a detailed exposé of the notion of *Gestaltung*, Stanford Anderson highlights this lineage between the installation of one of Maillol's sculptures by Peter Behrens at the Mannheim exhibition of 1907 and the permanent recurrence of sculptural bodies in geometric spaces of Mies van der Rohe (project for a house with courtyard, 1934, which also contained the sculpture *Méditerranée* by Maillol). 'Behrens and Mies, when they would debate issues of materials or architecture, seized on a basic mathematical conception, most often ill-adapted to the material form: points, lines, plans cannot be built. The De Stijl artists (and Mies van der Rohe in his works inspired by De Stijl) speak of lines and plans but allow for ambiguities in their assembly to complete the forms that neither their words, nor those of a mathematician can adequately describe.'[18]

This mathematization that enables one to keep *Gestaltung* within a rational and geometric framework flows directly from J.L.M. Lauweriks. Influenced, just like Piet Mondrian, by the theosophist philosophy of Dr M. Schoenmakers, Lauweriks was searching for a geometric transcription of the world inspired by this doctrine and trying to elaborate in progressive spatial diagrams the laws of spatial composition. His incessant research on the grid, as pattern or spatial object, which Peter Behrens, Mies van der Rohe or J.J.P Oud later claimed directly, is less the effect of a mastery of the plan through separations than a game of geometric progression. Lauweriks thus was seeking to formalize an order of movement and inflection also present in his drawings portraying the turbulence of war, entitled *Weltkriegsdenkmal*, 1915.[19] This rational quest, most often interpreted unilaterally according to a Euclidean geometry, later led many architects back to classical composition, an idealistic, formalistic and abstract order, which was nevertheless in contradiction with the dynamic of the Gestaltung. The development of a historical view of Modernism even seems to be limited by this return to order. Literature dedicated to the Bauhaus, notably Hans M. Wingler's work, eschews any reference to Henry Van de Velde concerning the first school in Weimar and his relationship with Gropius, while the expressionist origins of the Werkbund are greatly diminished. Graver still, two logics of the *Sachlichkeit* are distinguished here: that of the artists, open in a way to experimentation, and that of the architects, supposedly aiming only for the rationalization of the products of industrialization, and substituting the notion of 'good form' (*Die gute Form*) for that of *Gestaltung*. And yet, many artists and architects tried to open geometric space to a spiritual dimension, an issue that was even at the very foundation of 20th-century avant-gardes. The repercussions of the *Analysis Situs* by Henri Poincaré would have a very important impact on all fields of creation. Beyond the abstract fascination for the fourth dimension and its representations, those of Charles Sirato and his *Manifeste dimensioniste* (1936), for example, it is indeed the comprehension of a mathematical continuum of this type, of the possible formalization of a new cognitive domain that would bring together Marcel Duchamp, Theo Van Doesburg, Piet Mondrian, Kasimir Malevich, El Lissitzky, Richard Buckminster Fuller and others. From the exhaustive historical indexation undertaken by Linda Dalrymple Henderson in *The Fourth Dimension and Non-Euclidian Geometry in Modern Art*,[20] the central idea it proposes is that the issue does not lie in the definition of a new spatiality, an extended geometry, but in the approach to this 'continuum', which transgresses the contingent structure of space. As Henri Poincaré insists in *Le Continu mathématique* (1893), it is about going beyond the order of representation while simultaneously asserting that geometry with x dimensions does indeed have a real object. Poincaré, giving as an example the change in the state of an object or a body in motion, seeks to define a priori the relationship between the intuitive and the analytical continuum, and he does so by using infinitesimal models. Beyond the emblematic *Nu descendant un escalier* (1912) of Marcel Duchamp, the numerous studies on the body in motion, the photographic prints, on inflexion, the organic forms, which mark the research of the avant-garde with so many milestones, are never limited to a quest for new forms. László Moholy-Nagy demanded proximity, the immediacy of phenomenality, by reconfiguring the position, tasks and competencies of the 'designer'. 'The sea rolls up onto the beach, the waves fold the sand. The paint on a wall cracks, its surface becoming a web of lines. A car moves in the snow, the tyres leave deep traces. A rope falls, it creates soft curves on the ground. A board is cut, it allows the traces of the saw to appear. All these phenomena, caused by these varied processes, can be thought of as diagrams in space representing forces acting upon the different materials as well as the resistance of these materials to the drive of these forces. If elements, forces and processes participate in an optimum coincidence, one can speak of an "objective" quality. This indicates that "optimum" and "objectivity" never constitute a rigid formula.'[21]

Though all the artistic currents flowing from the avant-gardes preserved this internal contradiction of *Gestaltung* by understanding their form as an 'in-formation', it is nevertheless surprising that a neo-rationalist contemporary architecture should have so meticulously gone about erasing the genealogy of the concept to rely only on geometric formalism where the architectural order had to limit itself to measures and proportions. The minimalist craze, an architecture of reduction, obviously owes nothing to Mies van der Rohe and one has trouble understanding how the questioning of standardization or normalization of production never reappeared, either with the postmodernist wave or with the protagonists of deconstruction, as if the identifying status of the standard, the type, remained an unquestionable a priori of industrialization.
How was it possible that a rigged-together historical reading submitted to the revision of the Werkbund, the Bauhaus, made no mention of the platform of the Circle group, Moholy-Nagy's influence in New York or the publication of works by György Kepes, which served as school manuals for several generations of students? Why is there no curiosity about this internal contradiction that riddles the work of Max Bill, who, after his time at the Bauhaus, developed research on the elements of prefabrication? All of his work stands in this tension between an art and a concrete geometric architecture, also claimed by many minimalist architects, a deep study of the conditions for production of industrial design with the foundation of the Technische Hochschule für Gestaltung in Ulm, and, on the other hand, the incessant research on topology, with the rings of Möbius to lean on. All of this is to forget that *Gestaltung* also extends to and speaks of *Gestalt*, this pre-phenomenological current undertaken by Franz Brentano, in which he refers to the long tradition of the idea of *empathy* as formulated by Theodor Lipps – to which Peter Behrens refers as much as Hermann Muthesius – to then be largely taken up by German aesthetics – one thinks especially of Konrad Fiedler and August Schmarzow – and to end with its theoretical fulfilment in the work by Wilhelm Worringer, *Abstraktion und Einfühlung*, a recurring reference of the modern current.[22]

Anticipating the phenomenological concept of intentionality, it is indeed a question of describing the phenomenon of the joint constitution of form and consciousness, of seizing the intertwined threads of qualitative, physical, material and biological determinations leading to a form to be established. How is the constitution of singularities rightly organized, without maintaining the representative distance of a subject or the idealist a priori of transcendental schematism? The debates and research of non-standard architecture still hang between a seemingly irreconcilable alternative of an almost materialistic immanence claimed by Gilles Deleuze and the semiophysics of René Thom, open to all applications in the domain of computing. 'The fold not only affects the materials, which thus become materials for expression, according to different scales, speeds, vectors (mountains and waters, paper, fabrics, living tissue, the brain), but it also determines and makes the form appear, it makes it a form of expression, '*Gestaltung*', the genetic element of the infinite line of inflection, the curve of a unique variable.[23] For the philosopher, the fold is obviously not a topological figure; it is not an issue of abstracting levels of *structures*, but of plunging into the heart of the general phenomenon of self-organization. In a decisive article dealing with the specification of the notion of structure, Deleuze appeals directly to the mathematical concept of singularity as it is specified within the framework of differential calculus. Structure unfolds as process: 'a system of differential relationships of singularities corresponding to these relationships and tracing the space of the structure'.[24] When Jean Petitot draws a parallel between the approach of Gilles Deleuze and that of René Thom, he is attempting to formulate what a 'theory of morphogenesis might be *in abstracto*, purely geometric, independent of substrata of forms and the nature of the forces that create them', claiming 'a physics of meaning'.[25] Thus, non-standard logic appears as a tool for this formalization, this substantivization of indeterminate objects. It enables one to elaborate an autonomous, virtual, structuralist domain, capable of actualizing and validating any model of interpretation according to a new general hermeneutics. The entire American current of 'formal ontology' draws its inspiration directly from the *Gestalt* of Franz Brentano so as to update the laws of objective associations in the cognitive domain. This 'associativity' allows the person engendering it to dispose of a genuine topology of meaning, a 'mereology', whose formalization through non-standard models found an effective application in the field of artificial intelligence, then, by extension, in all the fields of biology, geography and sociology, ending up with the creation of diagnostic software programs as well as expert design systems.[26] The formal hermeneutics Jean-Michel Salanskis claims, beyond the semiophysics of René Thom, the extension of a 'non-standard constructivism', goes beyond the latest phenomenological forms of description, to focus on tackling only the rationalization coming from mathematical continuity, to the a priori material relationships. Referring to the non-standard analysis of Georges Reeb, he insists that the theory of models intervenes 'like a representative additive with regard to complexity ... The mathematics of continuity teaches how to understand from the approximate approach of the hyperfinitary excess of the discrete.'[27] The questioning that this opens up brings ambiguity, however, since it is confined to an unprecedented rationalism presiding over the logic of the constitution of the real rendered in a generalized domain of computing. Thus, the issue of a 'naturalization of phenomenology' is an ineffective screen for the project of logicization of intentionality.[28]

Non-standard architecture is connected at the edge of this redefinition of *Gestaltung*, where digital tools and their capacity for algorithmic calculation allow one to enter on a solid footing into the domain of a continuous formal schematism revolutionizing the logic of architectural design. Here, form becomes a morphogenetic a priori, the forms chosen to embody architecture being in a state for defining a singularity only in a continuum in perpetual evolution. And this is indeed what Greg Lynn means when he proposes the idea of inflection (*curvature*) as a method for integrating different forces, an idea that refers directly to the notion of the mathematical continuum: 'Producing a geometric form based on a differential equation is problematic without a differential approach to series and repetition. There are two kinds of series, one discrete, the one of repetitive series, and the other continuous, the one of iterative series. The difference between each object in a sequence is an individuated state critical for each repetition.'[29] Here again one finds the schematism of the continuous, which René Thom uses as a tool for interpreting mutations of life, those of embryogenesis, translating them geometrically as 'salience' or 'pregnancy', a return to the relationship of the objectile and the subjectile, demonstrative of the movement to 'singularization' and individuation.[30] There is nothing organic about the architecture of Greg Lynn or that of Lars Spuybroek; no form is transposed from the description of living states. Architecture is specifiable only through the structural breakdown of the space of the forms to which it belongs; it is self-actualizing only in the permanent gap between the movement that differentiates it and the always inadequate definition of its own position. Non-standard architecture can thus be broadened to the principle of continuity with the full procedural field of architectural production. It is indeed because it seemingly denies any reality of representation, of any objectivity, but by asserting a priori its use of algorithmic calculators that it engenders confusion as to the state of 'virtuality', a theme endlessly renewed by the said virtual architecture. The imagery produced by architects who would enter into a contradiction with the reality of the principles of construction is not 'virtual'. What is virtual is the a priori of a schematic domain of the non-standard, which can be self-actualized, or not, in the genetic definition of singularity. All of the literature on the virtual is thus subject to caution, precisely the caution that supports the traditional idea of a sphere of representation. Therefore, one must be wary of the idea of dematerialization, of a belief in the 'immaterial',[31] which supposedly accounts for the transition from the world of objects to the world of media, and which confuses within it all logic of production with the one of a technical mediation, or to follow Jean-François Lyotard, a language whose interplay constitutes the last refuge of an intentional normativity.

Non-standard architecture, by contrast, has established itself as a domain of unprecedented materialization because it takes form in the very heart of a formal schematism that today drives all sectors of human activity. Behind the popular representation of the generalization of all things digital is the actual implementation of a theory of models articulated with non-standard logics that animate a computational space that now stretches from the economy to politics, industry, knowledge production ... However, by accepting this widespread mathematization, must one also reconstitute a last normative sphere that would define at the heart of this schematism the last figures of an order, those of a morphological type and those of the structures for a formal semantics? The issue of positivism should be clearly stated, beyond formal ontology, and its optimization of artificial intelligence should renew the closed world of a rationalism whose purpose would limit itself to the unilateral quest for performance and optimization. How then can one imagine an open normativity, always anchored to the heart of the singular derivation? How can one build norms that only self-organize their intrinsic capacity of never shifting into the representation of their own order and, therefore, norms that would only retain from their own effectiveness their capacity perpetually to delegate their identification? This proposition, which could introduce a genuine structure for a discourse on architectural policy, a policy of a perpetually renewed effectiveness, already determines the programmes that are recomposing the growing diversity of architectural trades. To produce architecture, therefore, is to accompany and transfigure the data of a situation; it is to make, beyond any notion of programme, a moment of resolution appear, a singular field that organizes its requirement for a generic interrelation with a genuine semiophysics of context. It is in this sense that the diagram is claimed by many architects as a method of derivation, under the same unity, of the qualitative and informational elements of a most heterogeneous kind. The diagram returns to the function given to it by Deleuze, to a principle of singularization, an 'abstract machine', detached from any morphogenetic understanding of a physical order of matter. Ben van Berkel and Caroline Bos clearly identify this genetic character, which in the interplay of inflection mixes the two faces of the objectile and subjectile. 'The diagrams, rich in meaning, filled with the potential of movement, are carried by the structure, outside any specific spatial positioning. Understood as activators and triggers for construction, they are no more objective than subjective, no more anterior than posterior to theory, not more conceptual than contextual. The diagram is positioned in the operational, inter-subjective and process field where meanings form and transform themselves interactively.'[32] The internal logic of non-standard architecture cannot conform to an order other than the pursuit of a rigid orientation established by the play in the diagram, organizing, on one level, the necessity of the diagnosis and, on another level, the methods for realizing the architectural project. Architecture transfigures its unity, its synthetic capacity to gather together the two faces of the architectural project: the diagnosis on the one hand, the design on the other. The diagrammatic method takes up these two dimensions under the syntactical unity offered by the language of algorithms. On the one hand, the diagram provides inflection of a hermeneutic capacity, and this outside of any contextual sociology (which could be called deconstruction), and grants it, on the other hand, constructive capacity where the engineering resolves itself in digital translatability, which hybridizes all the tools of production. Indeed, any non-standard project can be immediately developed into variations of industrial production because it is subject to automatic translation, to conversion into an immediate feasibility at every step of the digitized chain (what Bernard Cache defines as 'associativity', by comparing architecture's current situation with the digital revolution in the publishing industry and book fabrication). This idea of a differential norm, of a 'normativity' that constantly shifts the principle of its representation, suggests a new set of principles, doubtless more relevant, for understanding Modernism's foundation. Le Corbusier, who worked for several months with Peter Behrens (1910–11) and who was unable to avoid the polemics of the Werkbund and also claimed the spirit of *Sachlichkeit*,[33] never allowed himself any abstract representation of the norm. Normativity remained riddled with the relativism of the *Gestaltung*, which perhaps allows us to restore the post-war work of Le Corbusier to this continuity, i.e., of Ronchamp or the *Poème électronique* and the Philips Pavilion. 'The standard is established on solid foundations, not arbitrarily, but in the secure knowledge of things motivated and logic controlled by analysis and experimentation.[34]

notes

1. Abraham Robinson, 'Non-standard Analysis', in *Proceedings of the International Congress of Mathematicians*, Amsterdam, North Holland Publishing Co., 1961, pp. 432–40. Abraham Robinson, *Non-Standard Analysis*, Amsterdam, North Holland Publishing Co., 1966.

2. Abraham Robinson's work had a strong, immediate and international impact, especially in France, where the mathematician Georges Reeb understood straight away its significance. Joseph Warren Dauben, *Abraham Robinson, the Creation of Non-Standard Analysis: A Personal and Mathematical Odyssey*, preface by Benoît B. Mandelbrot, Princeton, Princeton University Press, 1995, pp. 374–75.

3. René Thom, *Modèles mathématiques de la morphogenèse*, Paris, Christian Bourgois, 1974; and René Thom, *Stabilité structurelle et morphogenèse*, Paris, InterEditions, 1977.

4. Gilles Richtot, *Essai de géomorphologie structurale*, Laval, Presses de l'Université de Laval, 1974. Gaetan Desmarais and Gilles Richtot, *La Géographie structurale*, Paris, L'Harmattan, 2000.

5. Bernard Cache, 'L'Ameublement du territoire', manuscript, published first in the US under the title *Earth Moves*, Cambridge, Mass., The MIT Press, then in France as *Terre meuble*, Orléans, HYX, 1997.

6. Gilles Deleuze, *Le Pli*, Paris, Minuit, 1988, p. 26.

7. Ibid., p. 27.

8. B. Cache, *Terre meuble*, op. cit., p. 68.

9. Henry Van de Velde, 'Die Linie', *Die Zukunft*, no. 49 (Berlin), 6 September 1902. The text was reprinted in *Der Neuer Stil*, Weimar, Carl Steinert, 1906. On this analysis, see Kary Jormakka (Dir.), *Form & Detail*, Henry Van de Velde Bauhaus in Weimar, Universitätsverlag Weimar der Bauhaus Universität, 1997, pp. 68-69.

10. G. Deleuze, *Nietzsche et la philosophie*, Paris, PUF, 1973, p. 59: 'Nietzsche calls the will to power the element of the genealogy of force. Genealogical means genetic differential. The will to power is the differential element of forces, i.e. the element of production of the difference in quantity.' Henry Van de Velde, at the time close to Nietzsche, later designed the layout for the second edition of *Thus Spake Zarathustra* as well as the building housing the Nietzsche Archives in Weimar in 1903.

11. Siegfried Giedion, *Mechanization Takes Command: A Contribution to Anonymous History*, New York, Oxford University Press, 1948; French edition, *La Mécanization au pouvoir*, translated by P. Guivarch, Centre Georges Pompidou–Centre de Création Industrielle, Paris, 1980, p. 58. Curiously, Siegfried Giedion, who in this work achieves a synthesis of the development of the concept of *Gestaltung*, makes the indissociable link between determination of standardization and the mechanization of movement and initiates a genuine archaeology of inflexion.

12. Detlef Mertins, 'System and Freedom: Siegfried Giedion, Emil Kaufmann and the Constitution of Architectural Modernity', in R.E. Somol (Dir.), *Autonomy & Ideology: Positioning an Avant-Garde in America*, New York, The Monaccelli Press, 1997, p. 230.

13. Hermann Muthesius, *Stilarchitektur und Baukunst: Wandlungen der Architektur im XIX Jahrundert und ihr heutiger Standpunkt*, Mülheim-Ruhr, K. Schimmelpfeng Verlag, 1902. Little by little the notion of style becomes problematic and there was a search for a more *sachlich* vocabulary. The word '*Baukunst*' began to be used in place of the word 'architecture'.

14. Lothar Kühne, 'Henry Van de Velde und der Typisierungsstreit', *Form und Zweck*, no. 4, 1978, p. 39.

15. Walter Gropius, 'Was ist Baukunst?', *Flugblatt zur Ausstellung für unbekannte Architektur*, 1919, published in Hartmut Probst and Christian Schädlich (eds), Walter Gropius, *Ausgewählte Schriften*, vol. 3, Berlin, Ernst & Sohn, 1988, pp. 58-59.

16. The review *G: Material zur elementaren Gestaltung* was edited by Hans Richter and Mies van der Rohe. The six issues published from 1923 to 1926 define a cross-disciplinary editorial policy gathering dadaists, surrealists, constructivists and neo-plasticians. One finds in its pages El Lissitzky, Theo Van Doesburg, Walter Benjamin, Hans Arp, Friedrich Kiesler, Antoine Pevsner ... Detlef Mertins, who was preparing another edition of this review, emphasizes the coherence of the commitment of such a diversity of creatures: 'The first issue included "Realist Manifest" by Pevsner and Gabo of 1920, who declared that art should give form to expressions of life in space and time; the *Proun Room* of El Lissitzky for the 1923 exhibition in Berlin 1923, updated by Werner Gräff with a new generation of engineers capable of going beyond 'machinism' through intuition; and the creation of the project by Mies for a concrete office building in 1923 accompanied by his famous manifesto on the art of building pure presence' (Detlef Mertins, Introduction a to Walter Curt Behrendt, *The Victory of the New Building Style*, transl. from the original, *Der Sieg der neuen Baustils* [1927], Los Angeles, Getty Research Institute, 2000, p. 49).

17. Detlef Mertins, op. cit., p. 50.

18. Stanford Anderson, *Peter Behrens and a New Architecture for the Twentieth Century*, Cambridge, Mass., The MIT Press, 2000, p. 90.

19. Nic Tummers, *Der Hagener Impuls: J.L.M. Lauweriks Werk und Einfluss auf Architektur und Formgebung um 1910*, Hagen, Linnepe Verlagsgesellschaft, 1972, p. 88.

20. Linda Dalrymple Henderson, *The Fourth Dimension and Non-Euclidean Geometry in Modern Art*, Princeton, Princeton University Press, 1983.

21. László Moholy-Nagy, *Vision in Motion*, New York, Paul Theobald & Co., 1947; 1968 edn, p. 36.

22. One returns here to the important collection of texts on empathy in the German aesthetic of the end of the 19th century: Harry Francis Mallgrave and Eleftherios Ikomonou, *Empathy, Form & Space: Problems in German Aesthetics, 1873–1893*, Los Angeles, Getty Center Publications Programs, 1994.

23. Gilles Deleuze, *Le Pli*, op. cit., p. 49

24. Gilles Deleuze, 'À quoi reconnaît-on le structuralisme?', in François Châtelet (Dir.), *Histoire de la philosophie, idées, doctrines. Le XXe siècle*, Paris, Hachette Littérature, 1973, pp. 309–10.

25. Jean Petitot, *Morphogenèse du sens*, Paris, PUF, 1985 (see pp. 66–74). Jean Petitot, 'Rappels sur l'analyse non standard', in Hervé Barreau, Jacques Harthong (eds), *La Mathématique non standard*, Paris, Editions du CNRS, 1989.

26. Barry Smith (ed.), *Parts and Moments: Studies in Logic & Formal Ontology*, Munich, Philosophia, 1982. Barry Smith and Chris Welty, *Formal Ontology in Information Systems*, Proceedings of the International Conference on Formal Ontology in Information Systems, Ongunquit, Maine, ACM Press, 2001.

27. Jean-Michel Salanskis, *Le Temps du sens*, Orléans, HYX, 1997, p. 278. See also Jean-Michel Salanskis, *L'Herméneutique formelle. L'infini, le continu, l'espace*, Paris, Editions du CNRS, 1991, and *Le Constructivisme non standard*, Paris, Presses Universitaires du Septentrion, 1999.

28. Jean Petitot, Francisco J. Varela, Bernard Pachoud, Jean-Michel Roy, *Naturalizing Phenomenology*, Stanford, Ct, Stanford University Press, 2000.

29. Greg Lynn, *Animate Form*, Princeton, Princeton Architectural Press, 1999, p. 33.

30. René Thom, *Esquisse d'une sémiophysique*, Paris, Interéditions, 1988. See the first chapter, 'Saillance et prégnance', pp. 16–34.

31. Jean-François Lyotard, *Les Immatériaux*. Album, Centre Georges Pompidou/Centre de création industrielle, Paris, 1985. Lyotard proposes to substitute the idea of a figure-image for the figure-matrix. The message is no longer independent from the means; matter is 'in-formed': 'With the "immaterials" the assignment of an identity (thing, man, mind ...) to a structural pole seems an error. The same identity can occupy different poles of the structure' (p. 17).

32. Ben Van Berkel and Caroline Bos, 'Diagrams, interactive instruments in the operation', *Any Diagram Works*, no. 23, New York, 1998, p. 23.

33. 'Having placed architecture in this purely spiritual event of composition, I can easily understand why the doctrines of the *Sachlichkeit* are so inaccessible to my arguments ... We didn't feel the imperious necessity of being *sachlich* in architecture by respecting the objective conditions of the plastic' (Le Corbusier, 'Défense de l'architecture', *L'Architecture d'aujourd'hui*, special issue 'Le Corbusier', no. 10, Paris, 1934, p. 61). On Le Corbusier and the influence of the Werkbund on the conception of standardization, see Winfried Nerdinger, 'Standard et type. Le Corbusier et l'Allemagne, 1920–27', in Rut Foehn (ed.), *L'Esprit nouveau, Le Corbusier et l'industrie, 1920–25*, Berlin, Ernst & Sohn, pp. 44–65.

34. Le Corbusier-Saugnier, *Vers une architecture*, Paris, Editions Crès, 1923, p. 108.

new
babylo

new babylon

In 1956 the young Parisian filmmaker, writer and provocateur, Guy Ernest Debord, met the Dutch CoBrA artist, Constant Nieuwenhuys; the same year in which the latter began his extraordinary project for the first global city, New Babylon.

For Debord and a group of Leftist writers who formed the Lettrist International (LI), the city was a theatre, a place of infinite possibility and excitement. Drawing from the Surrealist idea of automatic writing, they mapped their wanderings in the streets of Paris, drifting between centres of ambiance. They named this practice 'psychogeography' and Debord's playful Guide psychogéographique de Paris reflects this new spatial understanding.

The Situationist International (SI), formed in 1957, brought together architects, writers and artists, including Constant. All were profoundly critical of existing architectural and social structures. In the immediate post-War era, the functional requirement of architecture to service reconstruction had led to a swift corruption of the ideals of Modernism. The Situationists passionately believed in the need for a radical re-think of society.

From 1956 to 1974 Constant devoted himself to the idea of so-called 'unitary urbanism' to create New Babylon, an urban proposition on a planetary scale. Anticipating the contemporary era of global communication, Constant's vast meta-city, realised in countless maquettes, drawings and photomontages, is populated by inhabitants who are constantly on the move. The artist famously declared 'we are all nomads now'.

In parallel, Yona Friedman, developed his manifesto: 'L'Architecture mobile' (1956), in which he too attempted to liberate the city dweller. His huge structures astride existing urban centres are iconic images of the era.

Constant Nieuwenhuys
New Babylon: Tour (Toren)
1959
Collection Musée National d'Art Modern - Centre Georges Pompidou

Guy Ernest Debord

> 283

GUIDE
PSYCHOGEOGRAPHIQUE
DE PARIS

ÉDITÉ PAR LE BAUHAUS IMAGINISTE
PRINTED IN DENMARK BY
PERMILD & ROSENGREEN

par G.- E. DEBORD

DISCOURS SUR LES PASSIONS DE L'AMOUR

pentes psychogeographiques de la dérive et localisation
d'unites d'ambriance

Guide psychogéographique de Paris.
Discours sur les passions de l'amour:
Pentes psychogéographiques de la dérive
et localisation d'unités d'ambiance
1957

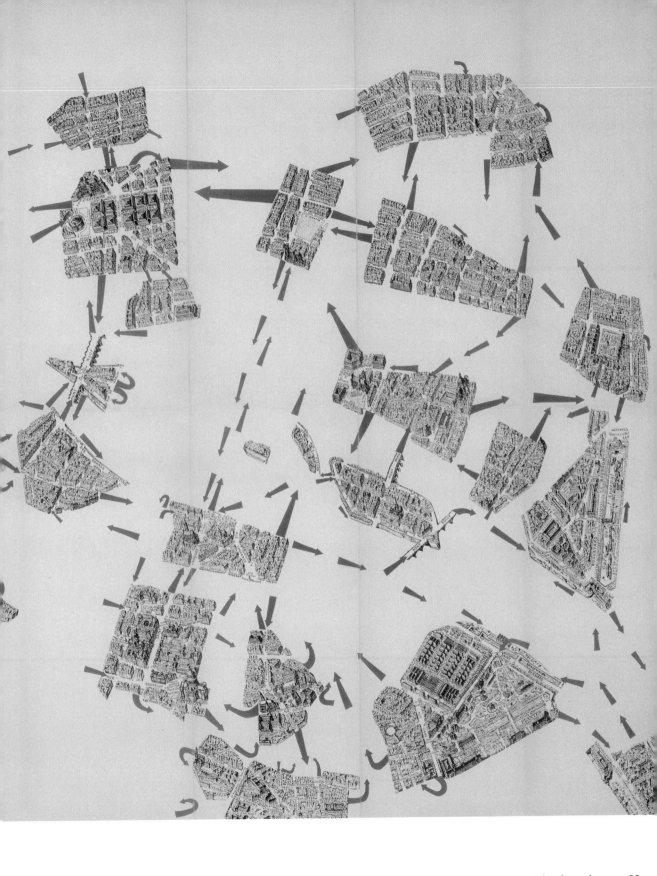

Constant Nieuwenhuys

> 280

Project for New Babylon
1956-74

View of New Babylonian Sector
1971
Collection of the Gemeentemuseum Den Haag

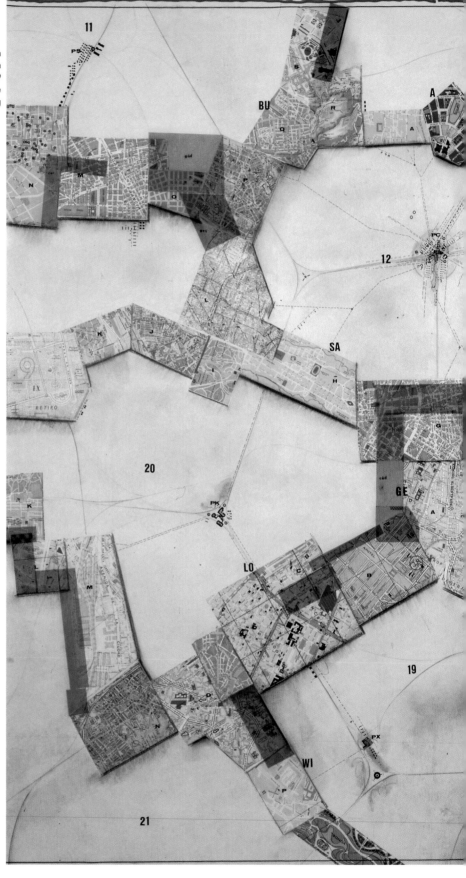

Symbolic Representation
of New Babylon
1969
Collection of the
Gemeentemuseum Den Haag

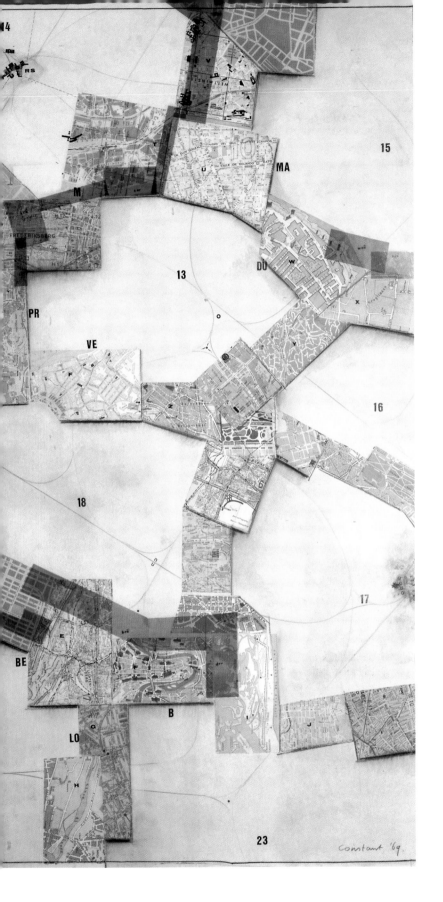

Constant '69.

New Babylon
1963

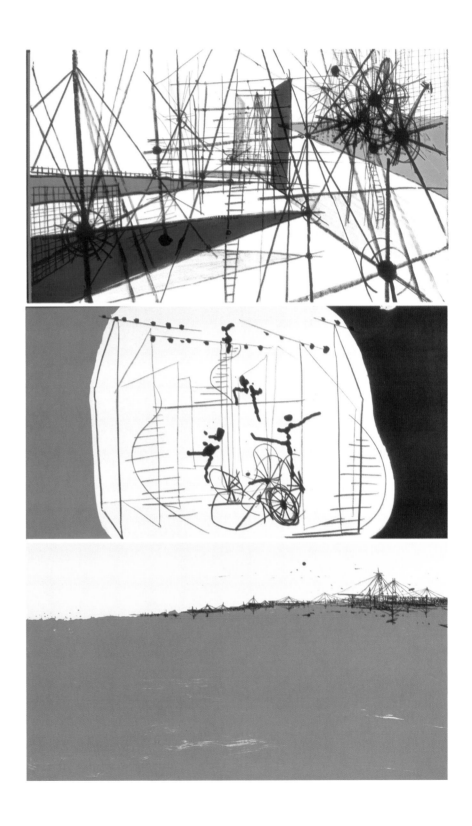

Yona Friedman

> 291

Spatial City
1958–60

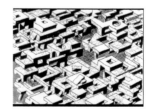

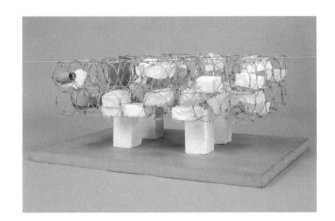

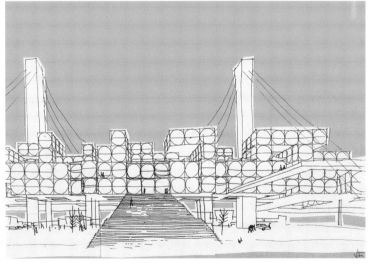

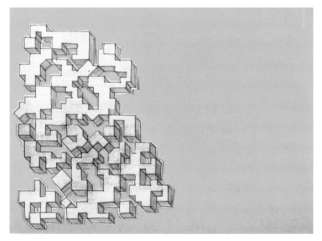

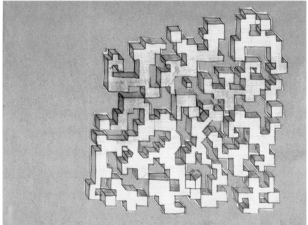

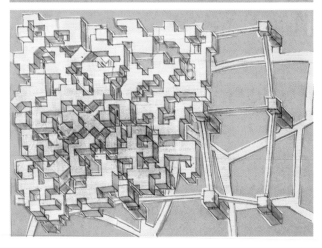

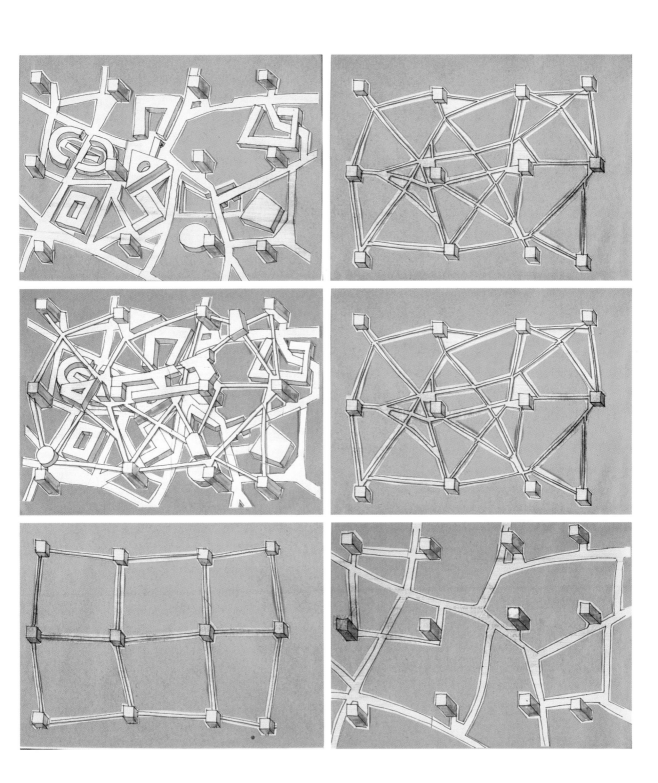

new
urban
habita

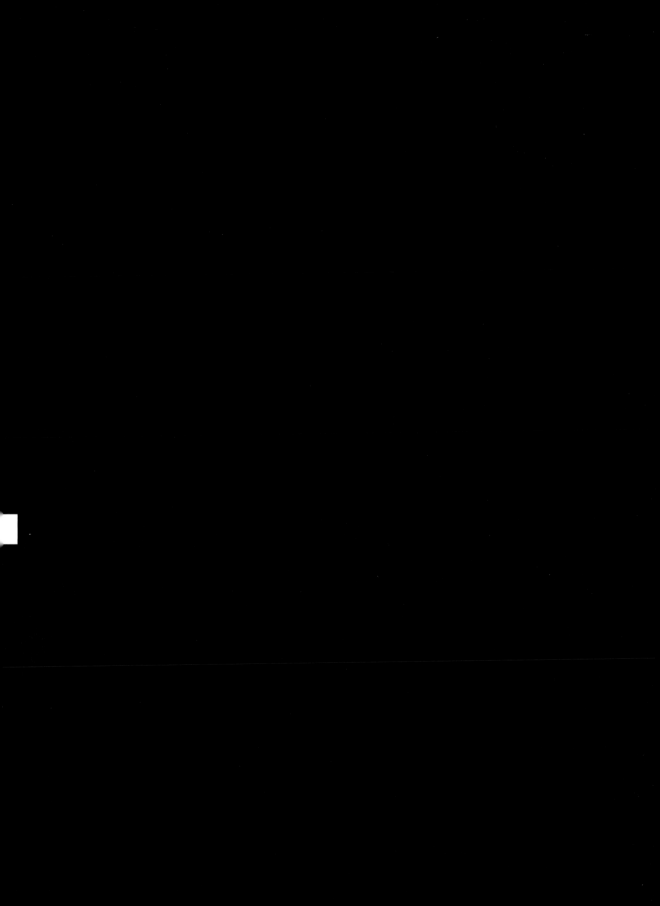

new urban habitat

The Second World War was a catalyst for the development of transient deployable structures. The architects of the 1950s and 1960s saw these technologies as an expedient way to harness factory methods of mass production, achieve economies of scale and propose new attitudes to human habitation and therefore a variety of new living situations.

One of the first was Alison and Peter Smithson's House of the Future (1956). Prefabricated, their visionary habitat developed the streamlined science fiction aesthetic that so many thought the year 2000 would have. Meanwhile Ionel Schein, David Georges Emmerich, Pascal Häusermann and Chanéac all produced work that sought to further develop the prefabricated, curvaceous aesthetic of the pod. Archigram's David Greene, created one of the most memorable. His Living Pod (1966–67) was intended as an inhabitable machine for wandering nomads of the space age. Greene was just one of those who sought to find and define new forms of dwelling appropriate to the time.

Alison & Peter Smithson
House of the Future
Ideal Home Exhibition, Olympia, London 1956

Ionel Schein

> 319

**Mobile Cabin Hotel, Le Troisième Salon International de l'Equipement Hôtelier
Paris, 1956**

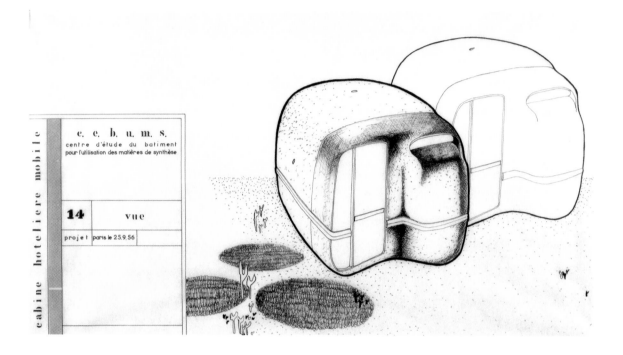

cabine hoteliere mobile

e. e. b. u. m. s.

centre d'étude du batiment
pour l'utilisation des matières de synthèse

14 vue

projet | paris le 25.9.56

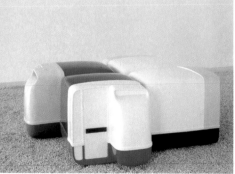

David Georges Emmerich

> 287

Agglomeration (Under the cupola of a space truss)

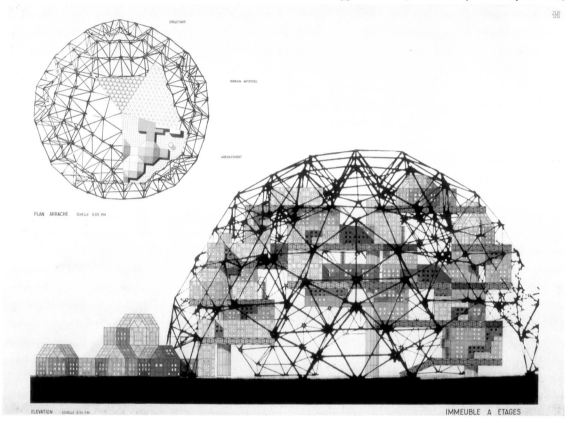

Project for Bateaux-mouches
1970

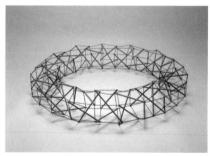

Structure Autotendante
1958–60

Structure Autotendante
1958–60

Alison & Peter Smithson

> 320

House of the Future
Ideal Home Exhibition, Olympia, London, 1956

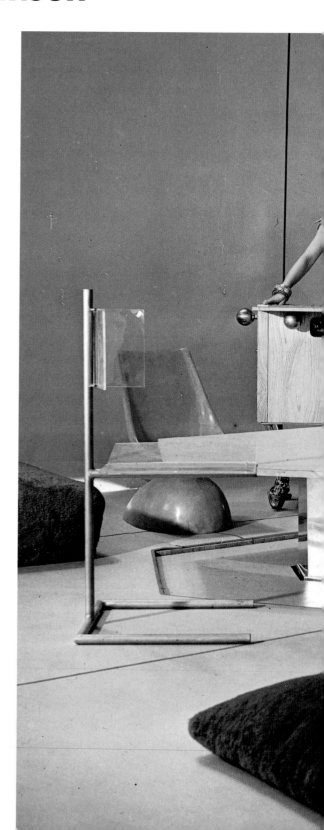

Pascal Häusermann

> 295

Spatial Construction
1970

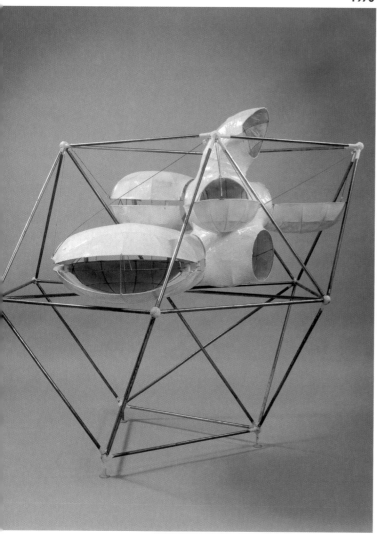

Project for the Habitat Denis
1972–73

Project for the Habitat Bérard
1972–76

Plastic Cellules
1968–69

Domobiles
1971–73

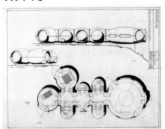

Chanéac

> 279

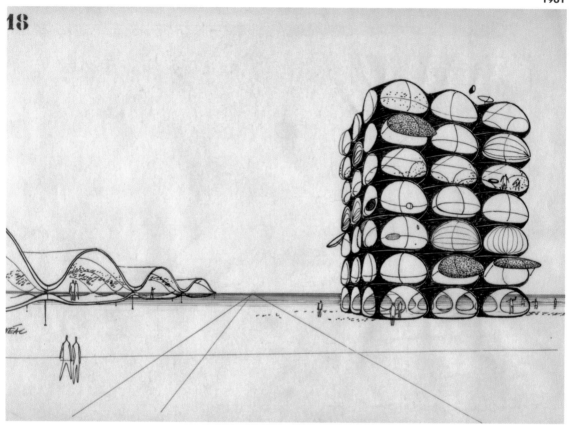

Cellules Parasite, Cellules Ventouses
1968

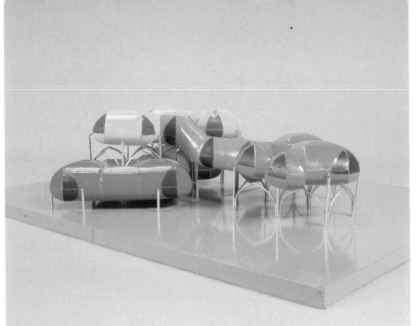

Study for Gothic Modules
1973

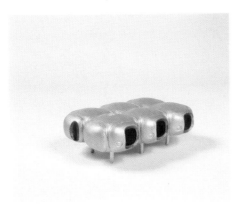

Amphora Cellules
1973

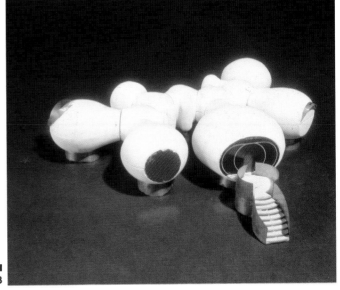

Amphora Cellules II
1973

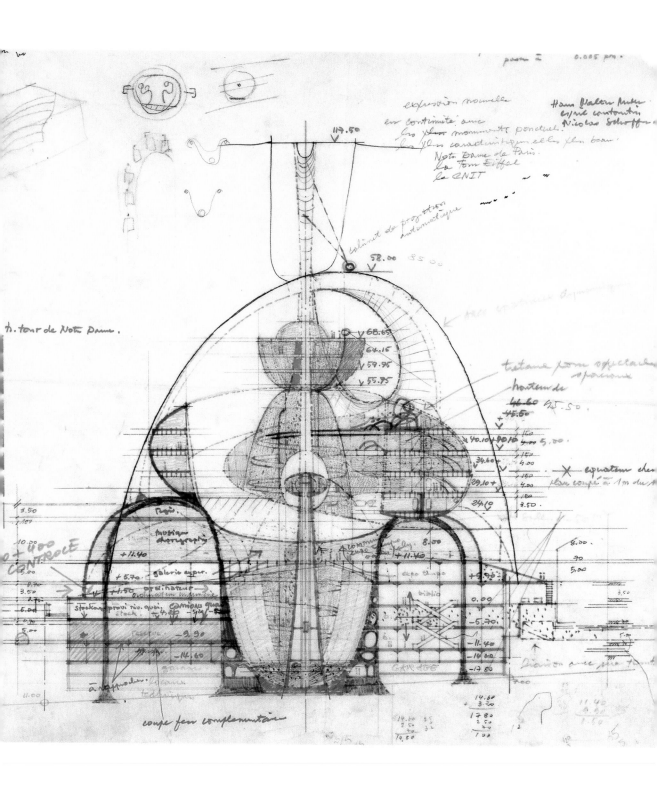

David Greene

(Archigram)

> 293

Living Pod
1967

organi
city

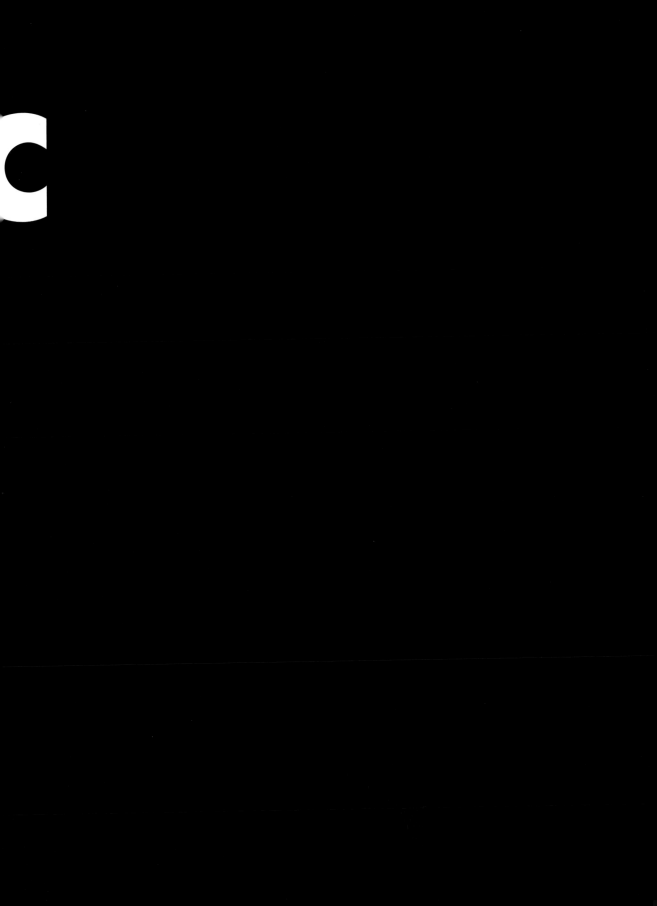

organic city

In the 1950s the Modern Movement's ideal of the integration of all
the arts became reactivated, particularly in the relationship between
architecture and sculpture. In France and Europe André Bloc fostered
a sculptural approach to architecture, editing the journal *L'Architecture
d'Aujourd'hui*. In England the editorial team of *Architectural Design* also
informed the architectural community of ideas that saw the city as an
organism with spines, lungs, arteries, skins and even erogenous zones.
Organic architecture, a principal theme of the 1960s, was characterised
by flexible, supple volumes and continuous surfaces. Some of these
projects were realised using new technologies for casting concrete on
a grid plan. In France, Antti Lovag experimented with this technique,
producing curvilinear architecture without any right angles. The Hungarian
artist and architect Pierre Székely created houses, churches and furniture
with abstract geometric forms. Architects sought inspiration in all manner
of organic forms and processes: Porro in the architecture of the lobster
and the human form, Lovag in the forms of abandoned pupae. In England,
Arthur Quarmby did some of the most interesting work with plastic
prefabricated modules such as his Corn on the Cob housing (1962).

Ricardo Porro
Ecole de Danse Moderne
Havana, Cuba, 1964

André Bloc

> 278

6 sculptures
Meudon, France, 1960–64

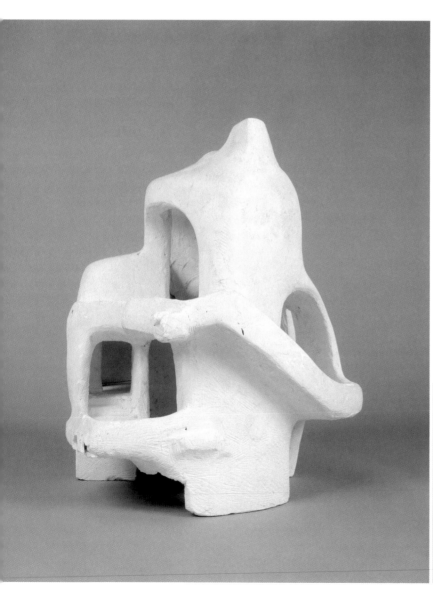

Sculpture-Habitacle
1962–64

Untitled
1960

Ricardo Porro

> 315

Ecole de Danse Moderne
Havana, Cuba, 1962–64

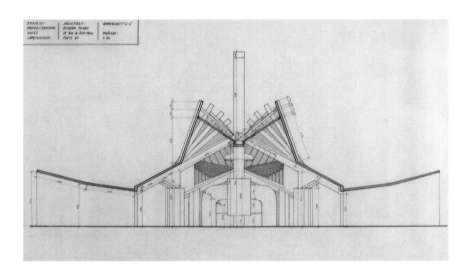

Youth Centre
Vaduz, Lichtenstein, 1972

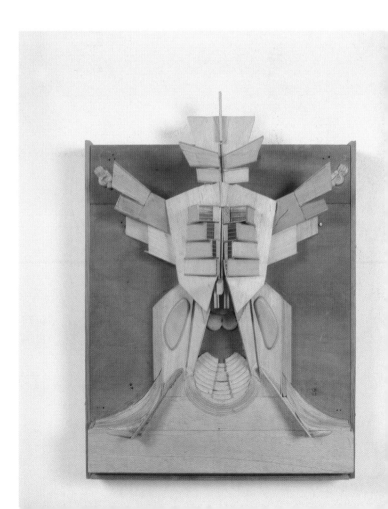

Antti Lovag

> 306

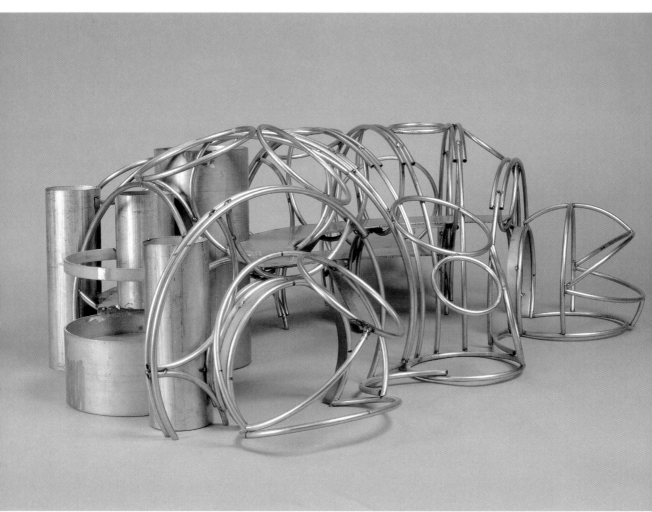

Untitled
1993

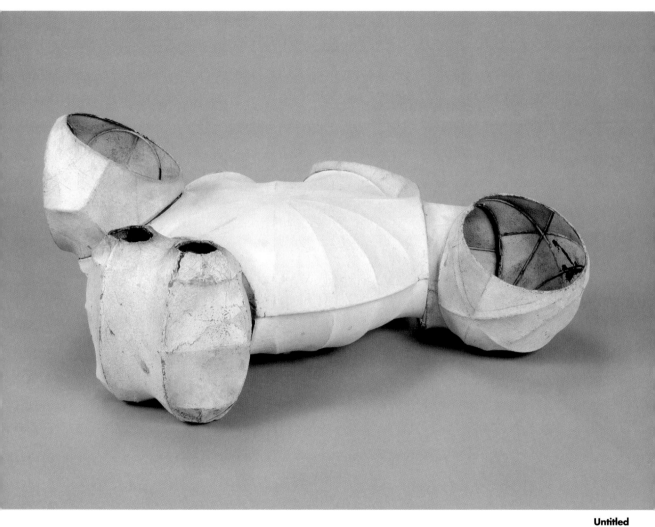

Untitled
1966

Espace Cardin
Théoule-sur-Mer, France, 1988–92

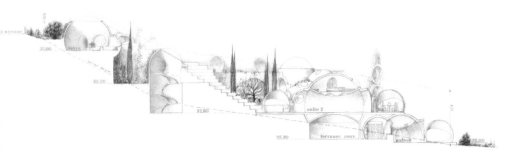

Vittorio Giorgini

> 293

Village, 'Futuristic Urban Scenario'
Ferrara, Italy, 1966–67

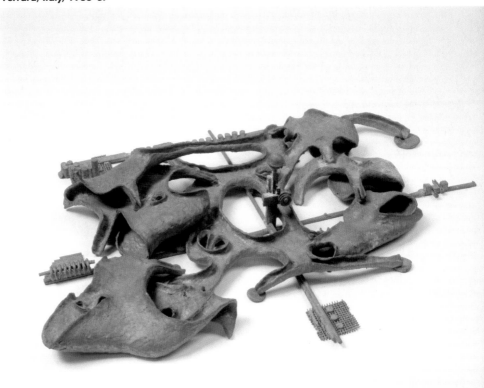

Liberty
1977-79

Liberty
1977–79

Pierre Székely

> 322

Le Bateau Ivre
Saint-Marcellin, Isère, France, 1952–53

Spiritual City
Rheims, France, 1962 (in collaboration with François Bride)

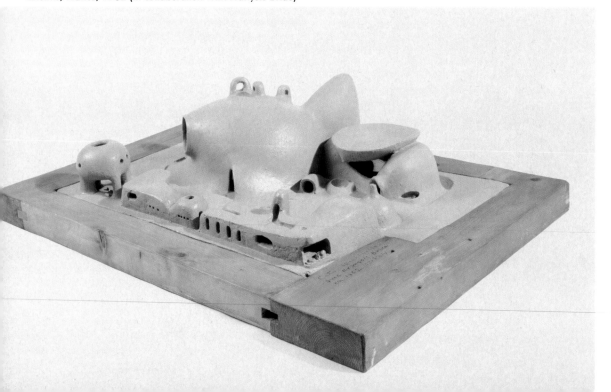

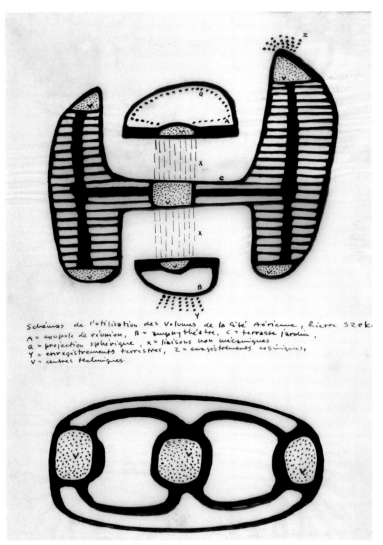

Schémas de l'utilisation des Volumes de la Cité Aérienne, Pierre Szek.
A = coupole de réunion, B = amphythéâtre, C = terrasse jardin,
Q = projection sphérique, x = liaisons non mécaniques,
Y = enregistrements terrestres, Z = enregistrements cosmiques,
V = centres techniques.

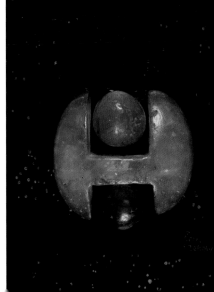

Arthur Quarmby

Plydom Housing
1962

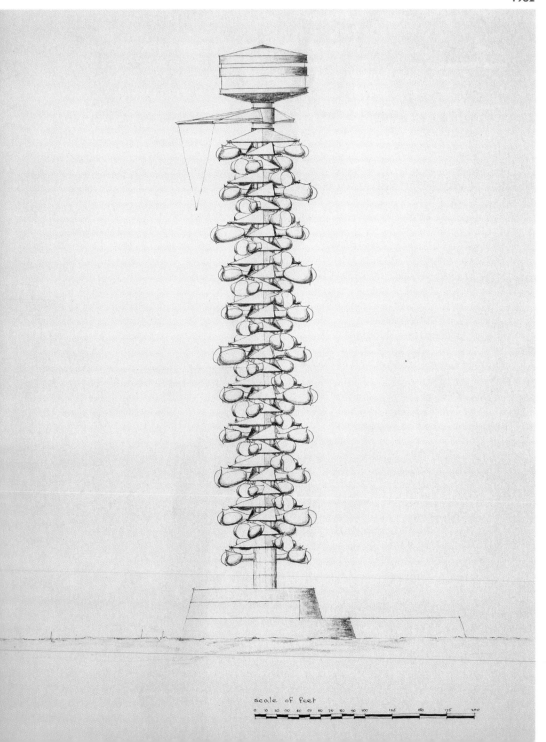

scale of feet
0 10 20 30 40 50 60 70 80 90 100   125   150   175   200

House and Garden
1964

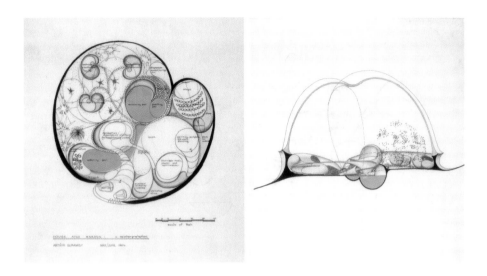

Brighton Marina
Brighton, UK, 1968

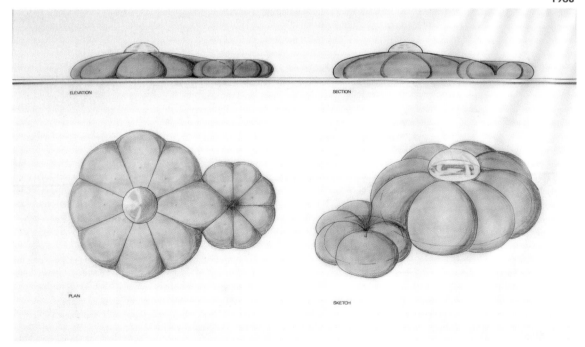

ELEVATION

SECTION

PLAN

SKETCH

inflata city

ble

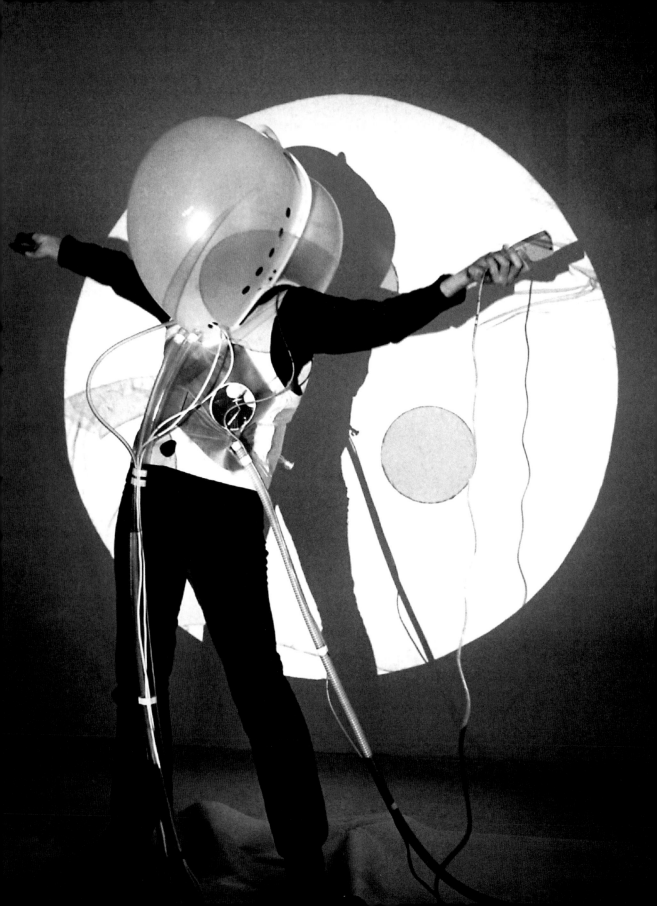

inflatable city

New plastic materials created possibilities for balloon moulding, and architects began to mould urban space as if they were artists. In Austria, Coop Himmelb(l)au and Haus-Rucker-Co made the city their main subject. In a model for Villa Rosa (1966-70) by Coop Himmelb(l)au, cells were grafted on to each other and moved from place to place. Here, architecture took on the role of a flexible interactive membrane that stimulated cognitive as well as sensory experience. In England, Peter Cook and Ron Herron's Instant City (1968-70) (Archigram) was an aerial city that attached itself onto an existing city and moved like an air balloon. This created a media event for the enjoyment of the general public, linking architecture to Pop Art. Graham Stevens produced the first inflatable structures, which appeared in the early James Bond movies.

Coop Himmelb(l)au
The White Suit
1969

Peter Cook & Ron Herron

(Archigram)

> 281

Instant City
1968–70

**Peter Cook
Instant City Visits Bournemouth
1968**

**Peter Cook
Instant City in a Field Long Elevation, 1/200
1969**

Peter Cook
Instant City (Rupert IC 2),
Airship Sequence of Effect of an English Town
1969

Dirigible Instant City M3
1969–98

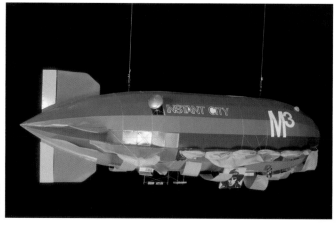

Peter Cook
Airship 'Zeppelin' Model
1969–70

Coop Himmelb(l)au

> 282

Villa Rosa
Vienna, 1966-70
(model 1967)

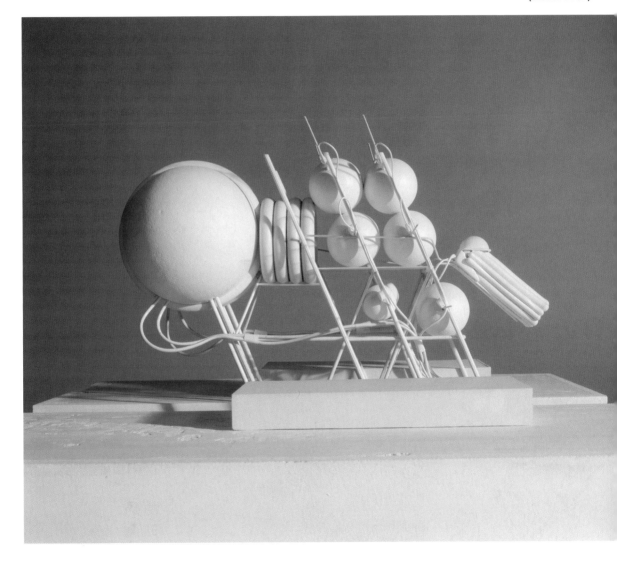

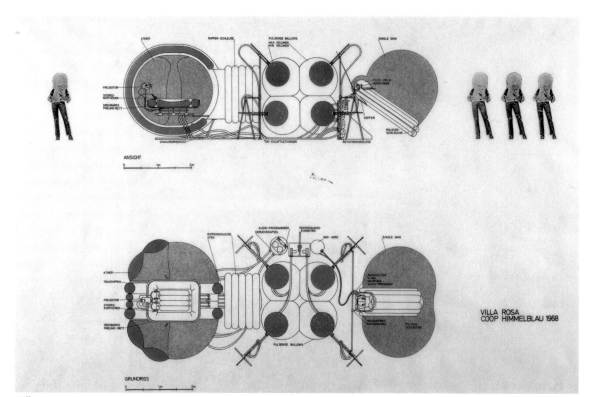

Villa Rosa
1968

Cloud
1968–72

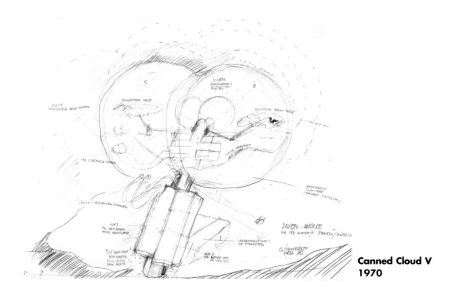

Canned Cloud V
1970

Cloud
1968

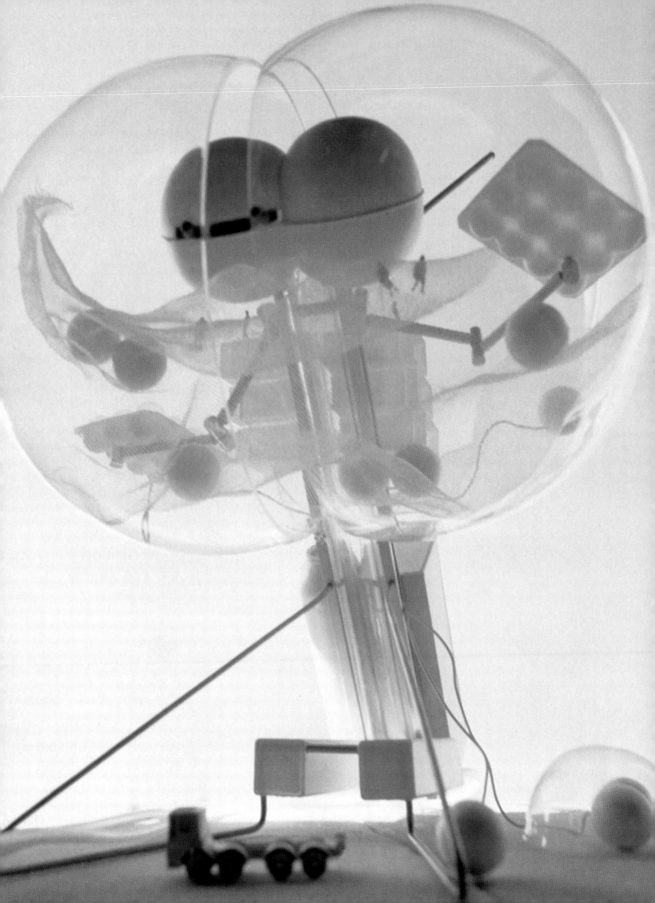

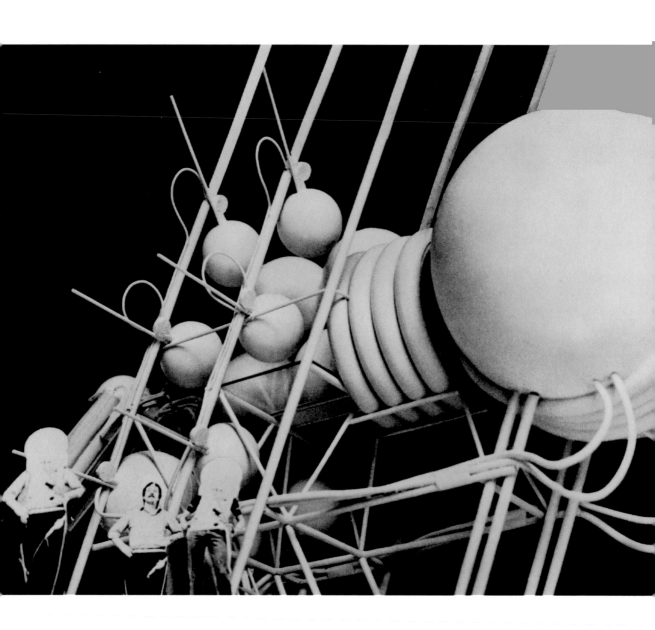

Villa Rosa
1968

Villa Rosa
1968

Haus-Rucker-Co

> 296

Pneumacosm
1967–71

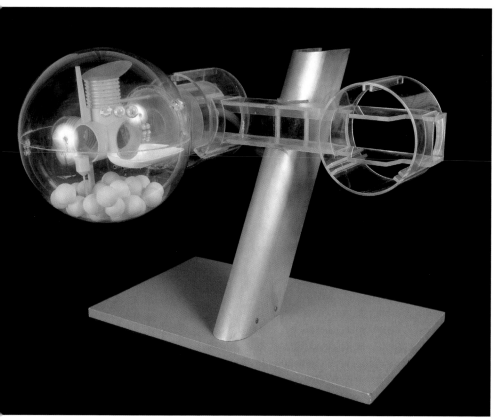

Pneumacosm
1968

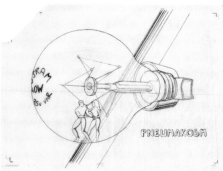

Pneumacosm Perspective
1968

Pneumacosmic Formation
1971

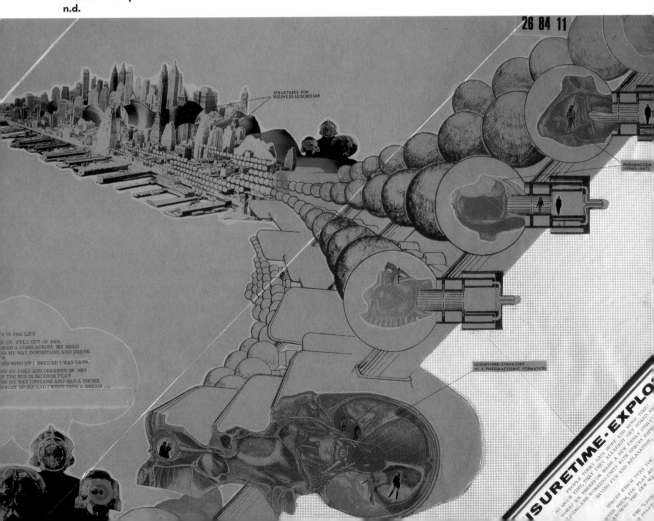

Overleaf. Oase Nr. 7
Documenta 5, Kassel, 1972

Leisuretime Explosion
n.d.

STRUCTURES FOR
BUSINESS-LEISURETIME

26 84 11

PNEUMACOSM
LIVING-UNITS

LEISURETIME-STRUCTURE
IN A PNEUMACOSMIC FORMATION

Y IN THE LIFE
E UP, FELL OUT OF BED,
GED A COMB ACROSS MY HEAD
GO MY WAY DOWNSTAIRS AND DRANK
P,
LOOKING UP I NOTICED I WAS LATE,
ND MY COAT AND GRABBED MY HAT
E THE BUS IN SECONDS FLAT
ND MY WAY UPSTAIRS AND HAD A SMOKE
EBODY SPOKE AND I WENT INTO A DREAM ...

ISURETIME · EXPLO
SO MUCH PEOPLE TODAY GAIS MORE AND MORE TIME!
WORRY TIME, THAT THEY ALLREADY GET BOARD W
LIVING AND WORKING-UNITS WITH SPACES THRO
HAVING FUN AND RELAXATION
BETWEEN THEM, YOU CAN PLAY A
HOPING THE TIME TO YO
THE "LEISU

Graham Stevens

> 320

Desert Cloud
1974

Flying in the Arabian Desert
1974, filmed in Kuwait

Atmospheric Raft
1969, filmed in Binfield, Berkshire, UK

Atmosfields
events filmed in 1969–1970

Raintube
1970, filmed in St Katharine Dock, London

megast

megastructure

During the 1970s the English architectural theorist and historian Reyner Banham invented the term 'megastructures'. It was to describe those projects that promoted the view that existing urban centres were poorly equipped to cope with contemporary urban living, mobility, technology and leisurely play. Megastructures were characterised by buildings on a massive scale, heroic structures to which smaller pods, capsules and partitions could be added or taken away: quietly relocated according to daily or hourly spatial demand. One of the definitive megastructures is Eilfried Huth and Günther Domenig's Ragintz (1965-69), a forerunner of large multifunctional buildings such as the Pompidou Centre in Paris. Chanéac's Crater City (1963) is contemporary with Constant's New Babylon and the difference in social prescription can be easily observed between the two schemes.

In Vienna, two radical figures, Walter Pichler and Hans Hollein, exhibited together in 1963. Under the influence of such exemplary conceptual projects as Pichler's Compact City (1963) and Hollein's Project City-Communication Interchange as a Means of Expression (1962), the Viennese school of architectural experiment was born.

Hans Hollein
Superstructure Over Vienna
1960
Collection Musée National d'Art Moderne - Centre Georges Pompidou

Hans Hollein

> 297

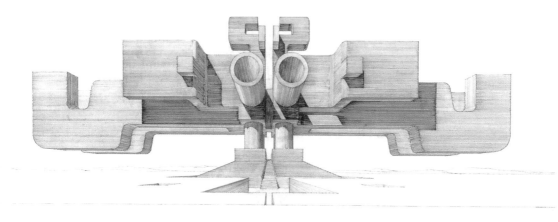

Project City-Communication Interchange as a Means of Expression
1962
Collection Musée National d'Art Moderne - Centre Georges Pompidou

Aeroplane Carrier City
1964
Collection Musée National d'Art Moderne - Centre Georges Pompidou

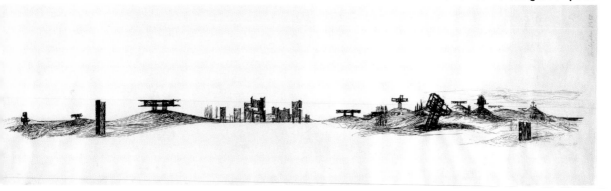

Eilfried Huth &
Günther Domenig

> 297

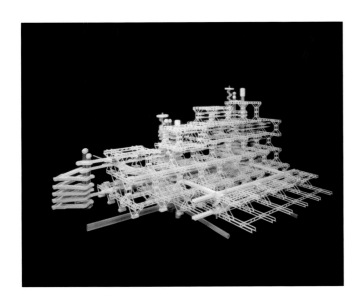

Ragnitz
Austria, 1965–69
(Model 2001)

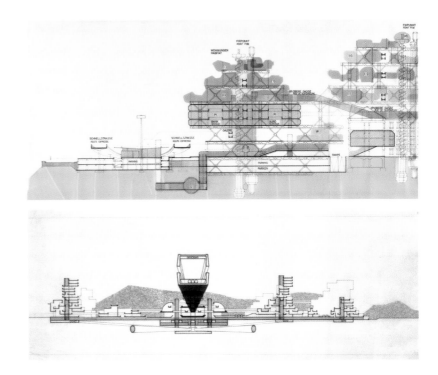

Chanéac

> 279

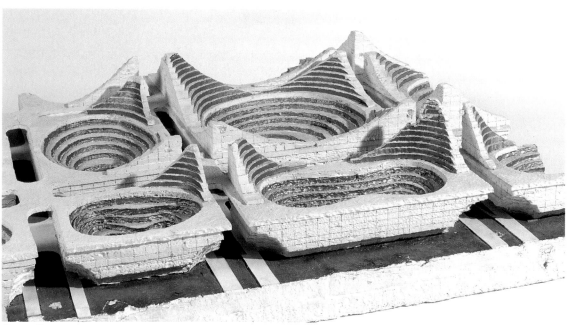

Crater City
1963

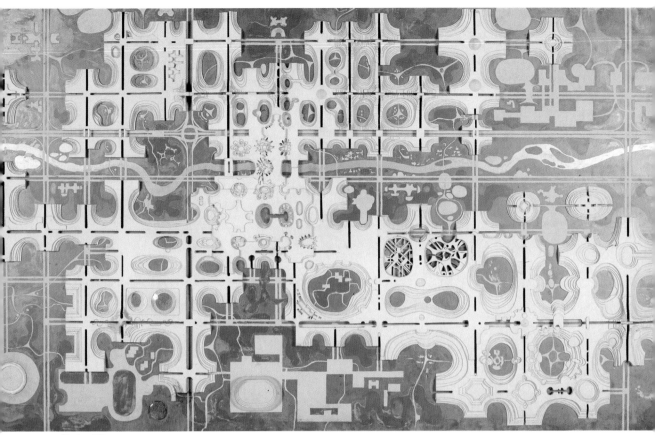

Crater City
c. 1968

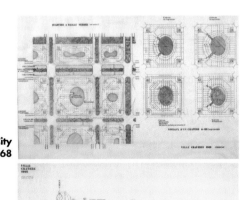

Crater City
1968

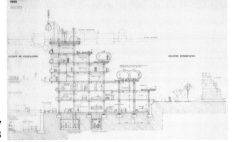

Crater City
1968

Walter Pichler

> 314

Compact City
1963–64

Compact City
1964

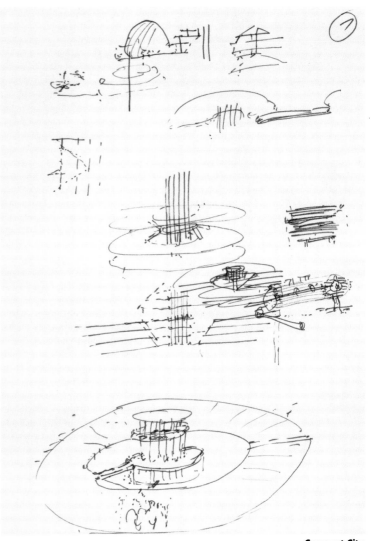

Compact City
1963

Compact City
1963

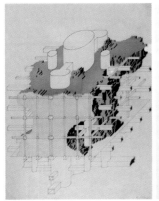

Compact City
1963

the
oblique
city

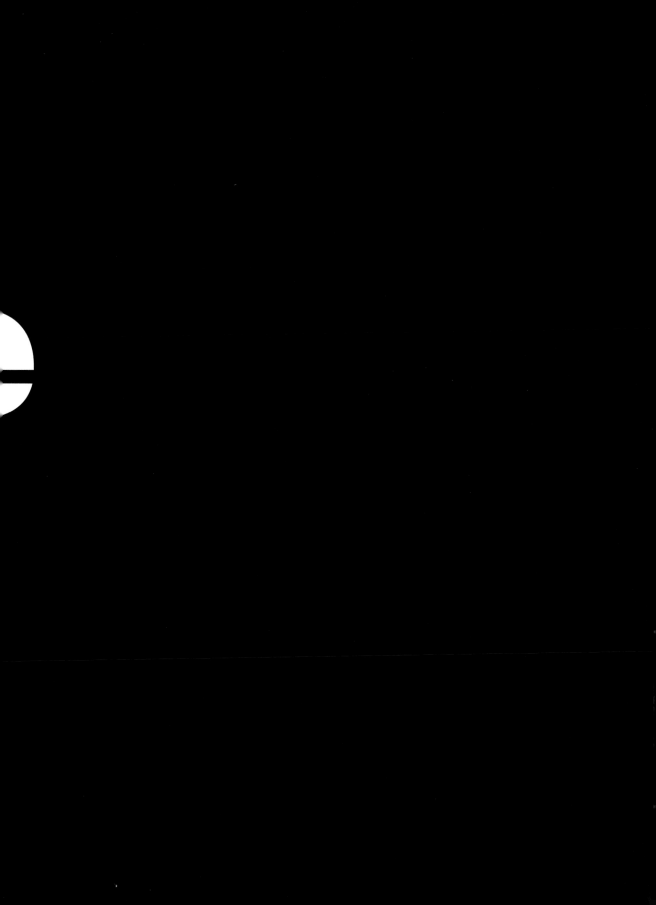

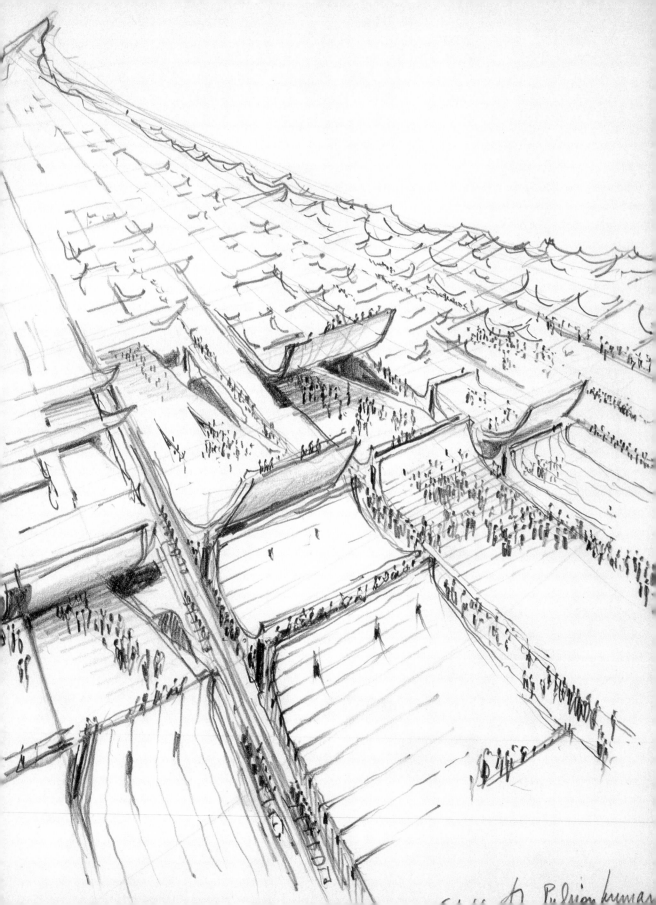

architecture principe: the oblique city

At the beginning of the 1960s, Architecture Principe (Claude Parent and Paul Virilio) published their theory of a sloping city, 'The Function of the Oblique.' Their tilting site was intended to stimulate and encourage human social activity. They saw the city as symbolic of all human civilization and characterised movement through it as circuits or cycles, equivalent to human habitation. For them, the 'function of the oblique' was a 'device' that would unify the physical movement of its inhabitants because their movement was made easier in extensive, continuous spaces. The research of Architecture Principe anticipated the work of today's architects who are exploring the folded forms that integrate the built and natural landscape and who use digital tools to create architecture that has an interactive relationship with its inhabitants. Equally, many of the works of Parent and Virilio are forerunners to later experiments conducted under the banner of Deconstruction.

Architecture Principe
Human Impulse
1966

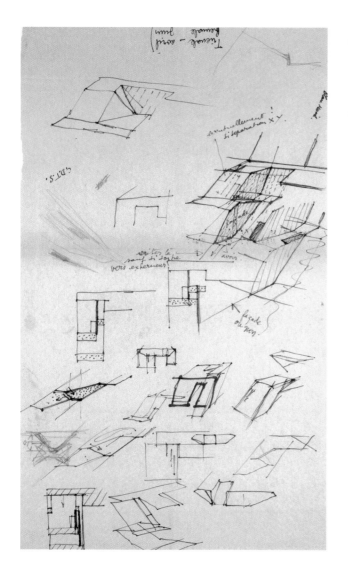

Architecture Principe

> 274

Maison Mariotti
1967-70

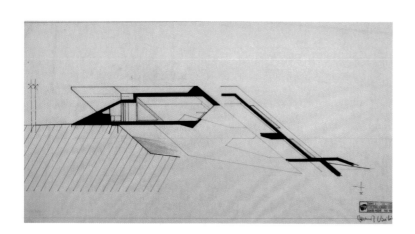

dominating the site

Architecture is not biological, it is creation. Architecture cannot be likened to an object, it is anti-object.

Architecture rallies. It is the very essence of human groups.

Architecture is not integrated in the site. It exists in itself and establishes with the landscape a qualitative and dimensional relationship.

In a state of crisis, architecture must offer the solution of safeguard and survival.

Faced with needs, faced with restrictions, versus the impossible, architecture must:

• Leave existing cities and promote new urban complexes.
• Dominate the site, become the equivalence of natural reliefs, change dimensions. Become artificial relief, landscape ...Faced with the uncertainty of the psyche, faced with anxiety, anguish, collective fear, the advent of violence, architecture must manage to tip the mentality in two key ways:
• Inclined planes of installation and use in space.
• The cantilever in the obliqueness of masses (the interior is dwelling, the exterior is circulation).

Architecture must never be neutral or indeterminate.

It must be active; man in architecture must be concerned constantly, take part in an action or a spectacle. He belongs to the continuity of architectural worlds (buildings to be scaled and vanquished).

Architecture in its approach, as creation, must not proceed by way of accumulation, juxtaposition, addition of the basic cellular element.

Its formal concretization, its materialization sidesteps the process of the modular built-up area, as it does the study of form. It is at the stage of the concept, the principle.

Its dimension projects it once again towards the monumental in a new spatialness.

Collective life, incorporated in the city, becomes positive life force and is no longer a threatening and unpredictable power. It does not dominate the materialization of the architectural form.

Architecture will re-become the domain of proof. It will be indisputable, undisputed. It will no longer refer to the domain of the avant-garde. It will be. People will recognize it as theirs. The other arts will find in it both coherence and reality.

Claude Parent

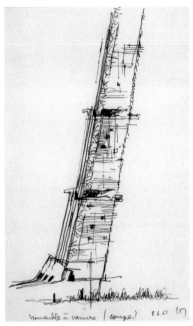

Building to Get over (Section)
1965

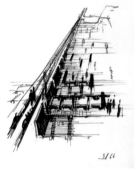

Untitled
1966

Building to Walk about – to Exchange
1965

the oblique function

If physical nature is typified by periodicity, the historical world is defined by polarity.

So the different units of human groups have been of paramount importance in the succession of urbanization methods and thence in the origins of architectural forms.

This process of polarization, which, out of some concern for analysis, should not be complicated by being developed, has hitherto given rise to the addition of individual dwellings, in the town, then to the addition of live-in cells in the building, duplicated by the addition of buildings in the city, each one of these successive units undergoing a change in the nature of its volume, followed by a total addition.

But these diverse modifications have been above all caused by a factor that has long been wrongly regarded as resulting from others: this is the orientation in space. If the village clearly represented horizontality in conquest of the ground, broken solely by the aspiration to verticality represented by the shrine or castle, the city has been nothing more than a succession of verticalities towards social conquest, and New York does indeed represent a culmination of this spatial direction.

If all attempts to reach a new type of urban unit have since foundered, be it the garden cities of 19th-century England or satellite towns, this is because those who have created them have misunderstood the predominance of an original axis of elevation as a driving factor of the unit's other components. They have been intrigued by the additional aspect of human groups, conditioned by the barbarity of the industrial civilization in its birth pangs.

Claude Parent

**Saint-Bernadette-du-Banlay Church
1966**

manhattan out

The industrial might that has erected its vertical monsters in Manhattan has proceeded in its entirety to the quest for mobility. The car and Ford may have been the symbol of the early 20th century, but the capsule and the rocket represent the achievement of this desire for both the object and the mobile.

Unlike ancient empires, the industrial empire has not managed to urbanize the dynamism of its conquests. New York, which is perhaps the sole expression of this civilization, fits into a dimension at its point of fall; it had come about from a mode at its point of culmination, it is the apotheosis and end of verticality, and American society can no longer logically go beyond this tendency except by launching its metal cones in Florida. Architecture for the USA stops where its rockets burst forth, and the efforts being currently made by that country to demonstrate its capacities of plastic invention in the field of sculpture and painting do not disguise the incapacity from which it finds itself suffering with regard to its architectural problems.

The old distinction between nomadic and sedentary still seems valid, as if a people also deeply involved in mechanicity since its earliest origins and in all its activities were, at the end of the day, unable to give birth to an architecture. The USA has merely managed technically to exasperate the vertical dominant of old Gothic art. A man like Frank Lloyd Wright always refused the city; his genius was an interior genius and his 1,600-metre/5,250-foot tower shows his inability to change nature while changing scale. As for the fondness for 'revival' and the lure of neo-styles, this clearly shows that after Wright's death and the very recent demise of Kiesler, American architecture is in the process of playing its last hand of cards.

Our day and age requires that architecture totally reinvent the city. Through the assessment of the city planner's leading role, and through the wish to conquer the old planet, everything that is beneath this level of ambition and appreciation will be useless and ineffectual. In the urban domain, we are involved in a drama, and it is for fear of destroying society that the deep-seated motivations of architectural creation must be re-invented. It is futile to dread scientific scourges; the hybrid place where we live and which lays claim to being a city is, alone, the source of a drama so extensive and so formidable that, to be done away with, it will require wherewithal and financing far greater than any national defence budget. New York, like a colossus dying from its insufficiencies, is the proof of this for us.

Shortages of water, electricity, mechanicity, problems of segregation, economy, security, the whole thing has a character emblematic of urban problems in the contemporary world. But an odd phenomenon of self-censorship comes into play whenever this tragedy starts to appear in its formidable continuity, a likely sign of the powerlessness of power and imagination.

Economic and social plans are concerned with the quantity and price of objects necessary for the 'comfort' of citizens, but in the field of architecture – that age-old art – it is on the level of quality that they should be set, i.e. of an answer to deep and altogether novel needs. We ask of the habitat much more than citizens did at the beginning of the 20th century – no longer just a roof, but collective clothing, the trampoline of activity, the cultural fabric, nothing less than an intimate stand-in for individuals. There is no longer any distinction between habitat, place of worship, place of passage, place of pleasure, place of work – it is the sole temple, which must contain everything.

All this calls for an extension of vision and imagination never before attained, which seems alien to the research of young American architects. So it is to sedentary Europe that we must turn. The cataclysm that ravaged cities during the Second World War has forged, for its conscience, a precise understanding of the urban fact and of the life and death of cities.

The phosphorus that destroyed Hamburg and London enlightened bright young minds. The city fatally appeared to them to be a whole, a unit. Ruined old façades have been the anatomy lesson for young architects; the return to the crypts of concrete shelters, an initiation to the origin of all architecture.

Now that its decline has been pronounced, New York can die, we have seen worse. In it, however, we salute the last vertical city, the completion of the second urban order. After the horizontalness of our old towns, the vertical order is dying in Manhattan.

Paul Virilio

inhabitable circulation

We have not managed to combine the solid element and the fluid element. Whereas, in other disciplines, the problem of fluids has long been solved, architecture, for its part, seems paralysed by human movement and this incompatibility between stop and circulation is in the process of destroying the modern metropolis.

In all its forms, the mobile has become the destroyer of cities – be it the social factor with its great mass movements or the various forms of energy used by industrial civilization or scientific weapons, not to mention natural agents, the modern city seems unable to master fluidity. In a world where everything is being transformed – objects into energy, points into itineraries – we can no longer dissociate dwelling from circulation, and henceforth two major trends will be pitted against each other: making 'MOBILE ARCHITECTURE' and 'INHABITABLE CIRCULATION'.

The first of these trends may take advantage of the word 'architecture', but actually borrows its case rom industry and consequently its means and its effects. The second trend, which might seem heretical, in reality merely has recourse to the very bases of architecture, in order to find the solution to problems of translation. We have too long regarded civil architecture from its protective angle and the stagnation of this art probably stems from an incomplete grasp of its nature.

It is no coincidence that real architecture has so often taken refuge in the staircase, the bridge, the dam or the highway intersection. In these things it found an exercise; whereas, in the habitat, it remained condemned to the most total passivity. Throughout time, architecture has found its accomplishment only when confronted and affronted by another power, be it spiritual or material. This art of power can actually yield its full measure in the exercise of this power only when faced with another sort of power. The embryonic industrial society of the beginning of the 20th century still did not represent sufficient power to give rise to a truly valid civil architecture. Today, the mass of people is such that it forms a force of unimaginable inertia.

So all the conditions are henceforth met for a civil architecture to be finally able to reveal itself, and for this art of space to accede to its true role, by shifting from the private domain to the pubic domain – the invention of society.

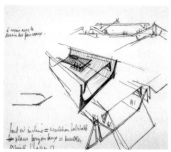

All Is Inclined = Habitable Circulation
Horizontal Plans = Furnished
1966

The Three Types of the Oblique Circulation
1965–67

There is no longer any question of architecture limiting itself to accompanying circulation or, worse, identifying with it by losing its specific nature. It is necessary to come up with a form of urbanism where circulation will become inhabitable, an architecture where the oblique function of animation will get the better of the neutralizing function represented by the permanent horizontal plane, an architecture where man will be set in motion by the very profile of his habitat, where the city will thus become a huge projector, a cascade for all activities and all fluidities.

This means the 'contraction' of the two major roles of this art and not a 'confusion', as is the case with mobile architecture. We have too long separated circulation from stop, and if vertical order has led to façade art and highlighted the visualization of architecture to the detriment of its effectiveness, horizontal order had previously denatured its use by straitjacketing it within stability and concealment.

Tomorrow, architecture will be essentially circulatory, the parking space will lose its importance in favour of the transfer space: the habitat, like the entire city, will be 'mobilized' by the oblique function.

Paul Virilio

fluidity

The oblique is the medium of spatial continuity. It is continuity. Its development helps towards partitioning without ever working against displacement or movement. As a structural medium, the oblique is thus associated with all movement of fluids generated by either man or nature.

The inclined site offers the element of water a maximum receiving surface, getting rid of the unusable vertical surface and developing a contact surface greater than that of the horizontal projection of the place.

The oblique function conveys its potential to water: catchment, storage and channelling all help man to create in 'sites' the spectacle-function fusion of the liquid element without mechanical intervention.

The inclined site is integrated in the element of air. By refusing to create general turbulence, the way very tall vertical architecture does, it nevertheless establishes, within the continuity of the rising dynamic of wind, a resistance, a permanent friction, which wears away the movement through all the angles available. The oblique function may venture into the field of acoustics, but above all it determines a new stato-dynamism where the fluid moves over architecture, which, without shifting, reinvents mobility.

The oblique function pits the ravages of the element of fire against the extreme development of its course, the great variety of its accesses and its flights, the rupture of the cuttings of its major lengthwise axes, the simplicity of its techniques and the dynamics of water.

The inclined site gives a person in motion potential and the complex choice of itinerary, the freedom of the route and the spontaneity of the gathering. This freedom from all manner of restriction will only increase in the future, because of the development both of the earth surfaces on the upper side of the 'site' and of the overhanging cusps of the lower side.

The incline precedes the human fluidity of the future, based on autonomous human flight. It is a gesture of linkage with space.

Claude Parent

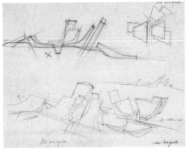

The Waves, the Circus
1965–67

Untitled
1965–67

The Cosmos in Waves
1965–67

the mediated city

An involvement with urbanism and city planning means dealing with an atmospheric layer in relation to a lithospheric segment, by therein creating relative and mediate structures. Unfortunately, for most city planners, the elevation does not appear to have exceeded its primary definition of 'occupation density'. The real scandal of a spatial dimension regarded solely as a 'means of storage' must appear to us in all its obviousness. This definition, possibly coming to us from the antiquated rural world, lies at the root of an astonishing fact: the identity of underground and above-ground inhabitable structures. It is actually noteworthy that in shifting from an opaque and solid element to a transparent and gaseous element, the usual space gains nothing more than a window opening.

It would thus seem that we should admit the paradox of an art of space, hitherto non-spatialized, in its effects, and in its consequences for man. The inability to conceive, be it above or below the skyline, of distinct areas of exercise for architecture, is there, if we still had any doubts, to provide us with proof.

The reference to the ground must shed this absolute and underpinning character that it still retains, to accede to a new definition where the ground is no longer regarded just as a 'watershed' between two specific spaces, between two particular natural states. Henceforward, it can no longer be the 'plinth of verticality'; it must become the 'axial line' of the architectonic exercise.

While vertical erection had just three possibilities – 1, raising; 2, elongating; 3, shifting – the oblique 'surrection' offers a host of possibilities through its gradients and their countless combinations.

What is thus involved is no longer incorporating in the ground 'targets' with an urban concentration caused by an immediate centrality, or with accumulation by an equal immediate verticality; it is important to produce mediate structures, at once circulatory and inhabitable, organized in tensorial clusters, unfolding and unfurling above the regions and vital axes of a territory, a layering of uses, depending on the needs of time and the masses. OVERCOMING and LIBERATING are thus shown to be the basic terms of the new urbanization.

Just when the levels of physical restriction are increasing, and just when alienation has become a common risk, we owe it to ourselves to ensure maximum development, for the inhabitant, of space-using capacities, by way of the slope, the curve and the topological or, rather, TOPOTONIC itinerary.

Paul Virilio

Reversed Simple Continuity
1965

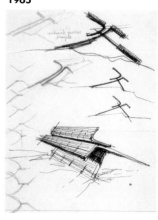

Untitled
1965

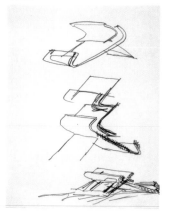

The Fault
1965

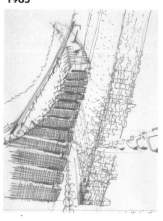

Les Turbosites I
1965

the
metab

olists

the metabolists

Japan hosted the World Design Conference in 1960 and here Noboru
Kawazoe launched the avant-garde Metabolism group. Founding
members included Masato Otaka, Kiyonori Kikutake, Kisho Kurokawa
and Fumihiko Maki, as well as designers Kenji Ekuan and Kiyoshi Awazu.
The group published 'Metabolism', a booklet that connected the
metabolism of living creatures with that of architecture and the city. They
saw the metropolis as being in a constantly changing state of dynamic
equilibrium, in the same way as a living organism. Their main objective
was to create structures that could expand infinitely. They achieved this by
designing megastructures that had capsules as minimum dwelling units.
Part of the zeitgeist that included Yona Friedman's Spatial Cities and
Archigram's Plug-in City, the Metabolists frequently proposed visionary
schemes for floating or aerial metropolises.

Kenzo Tange's Plan for Tokyo (1960), which put forward a vast extension
of the city out into the centre of Tokyo Bay, was an inspiration to his
younger colleagues Arata Isozaki and Kisho Kurokawa and is regarded
as having sparked the Metabolist movement.

The achievements of the Metabolists laid the foundation for much
subsequent urban development, and the breadth of their importance
is being recognised again today.

Kiyonori Kikutake
Marine City
1963

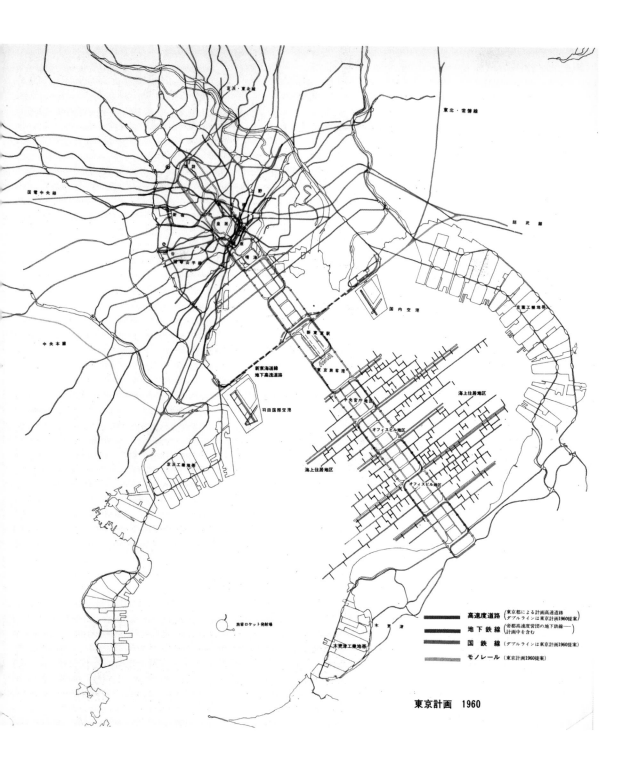

東京計画　1960

Kenzo Tange

> 322

A Plan for Tokyo
Towards Structural Reorganization Proposal
Tokyo, Japan, 1960

Yamanashi Press and Broadcasting Centre
Kofu, Japan, 1961-66
Collection Musée National d'Art Moderne - Centre Georges Pompidou

Kiyonori Kikutake

> 301

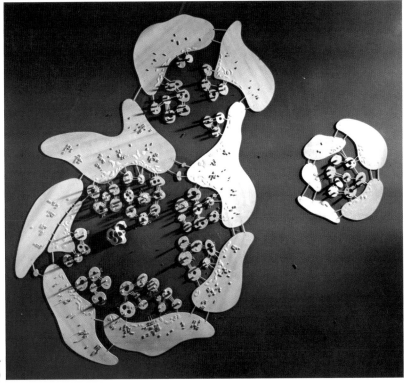

Marine City
1958–63 (Model 1963)

Marine City
1968

International Ocean Exposition
Okinawa, Japan, 1975

Aquapolis
1975

Expo Tower
The Japan World Exposition '70
Osaka, 1970

Kisho Kurokawa

> 304

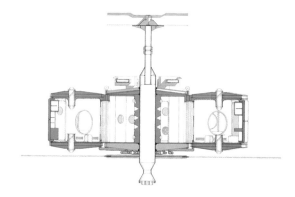

**Capsule House in the Theme Pavilion
The Japan World Exposition '70
Osaka, 1970
Collection Musée National d'Art Moderne - Centre
Georges Pompidou**

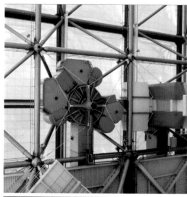

Floating City, Kasumigaura
Kasumigaura, Japan, 1961
Collection Musée National d'Art Moderne - Centre Georges Pompidou

Project for Box-type
Mass-produced Apartments
1962
Collection Musée National d'Art Moderne
- Centre Georges Pompidou

Arata Isozaki

> 298

Left. Incubation Process
1968
Collection Musée National d'Art Moderne - Centre Georges Pompidou

Clusters in the Air
1960–62 (Drawing 1991)

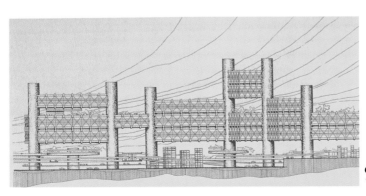

City in the Air – Shinjuku Project
1960–61 (Drawing 1990)

radical
archite
in italy

cture

radical architecture in italy:
superstudio and archizoom

According to art critic Germano Celant, Florence in the late 1960s was the cradle of radical Italian architecture. This movement was inaugurated by the exhibition 'Superarchitecture', held in Modena in 1966, and came to an end with the exhibition, 'Italy: The New Domestic Landscape' held at New York's MoMA in 1972. As successors to Pop Art, Italy's 'radical school' shared with arte povera the use of installations and appropriations from every day life. Superstudio's Histograms of Architecture and Archizoom's No-Stop City (1969) were derived from the Modernist concept of the uniform grid. But it extended into an idea of total global urbanisation through an infinitely spreading urban system. Through this threatening idea, architecture was seen as a socially critical act. Its identity was debated and it became regarded as an attempt to transform reality. Inspired by Guy Debord's Situationism, Superstudio were critical of the ubiquitous nature of global capitalism, a very current concern.

Superstudio
Monumento continuo con de Maria
c.1969
Collection Musée National d'Art Moderne - Centre Georges Pompidou

Archizoom Associati

> 275

Letti di sogno (Dream Beds), Imperial Rose Series
1967–2000

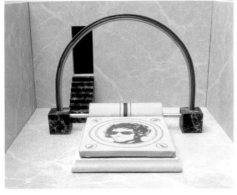

Distress of Rose
1967–2000

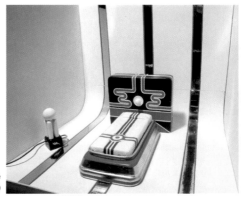

Electro Rose
1967–2000

Prophecy of Rose
1967–2000

Rose of Arabia
1967–2000

No-Stop City
1969–72

Superstudio

The Continuous Monument: An Architectural Model for Total Urbanization
1968–69

Motorway
1969
Collection Musée National d'Art Moderne - Centre Georges Pompidou

Il monumento continuo Paise d'o 'sole
1969
Collection Musée National d'Art Moderne - Centre Georges Pompidou

Overleaf. New York of Brains
c.1971
Collection Musée National d'Art Moderne - Centre Georges Pompidou

the
deliriou
metrop

us
olis

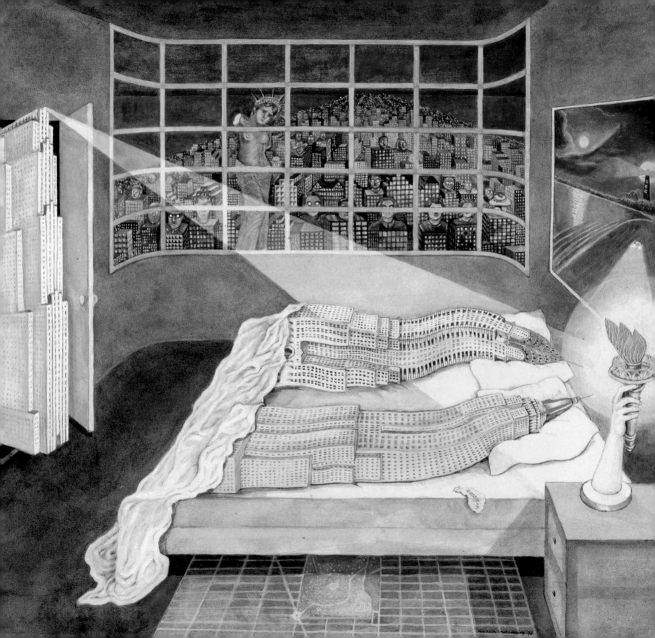

rem koolhaas: the delirious metropolis

Whilst most of his contemporaries were developing their proto-deconstructivist projects, Dutch architect, Rem Koolhaas made contemporary New York his focus, attempting to trace, distil and retrospectively extract the essence of this great city. He saw that most cities have a changing use pattern over time and that buildings can be catalytic to others. Equally, skyscrapers can entertain many functions and enjoy almost surreal spatial juxtapositions in their many stacked floor plates. He also recognised that certain parts of the city are informed with a peculiar history and genus loci that resonates through time, informing names and spaces of what comes after. Koolhaas' retrospective manifesto, 'Delirious New York' (1978) explained these notions, illustrating his thesis on the living body of New York, whilst also proposing new eclectic architectural forms to add to New York's own. He beds his visionary zeal for the future city in a deep understanding of how the metropolis grows, consumes, shops, relaxes and re-digests itself.

Exodus or The Voluntary Prisoners of Architecture (1972) is the first project undertaken by the original OMA (Office for Metropolitan Architecture) team. Here, Koolhaas and his contemporaries, Elia Zenghelis, Madelon Vriesendorp and Zoe Zenghelis, divide London by a huge wall into zones of 'haves' and 'have nots', creating a fictional narrative of wealth, consumption and disaffection.

Rem Koolhaas
Flagrante Delicto
1975

Rem Koolhaas

> 302

Illustration for the book Delirious New York
Thames & Hudson, London, 1978

The City of the Captive Globe
1972

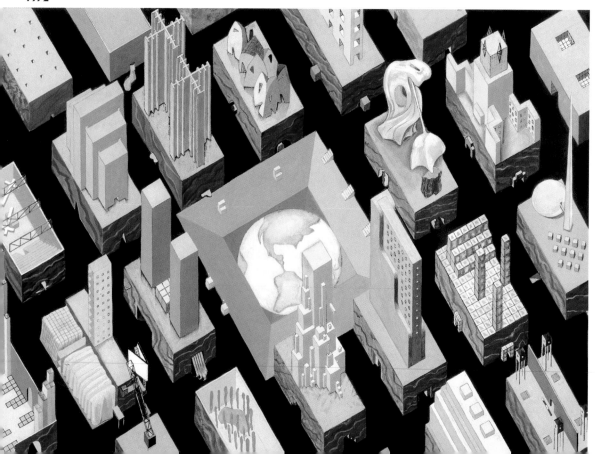

New Welfare Island
1975

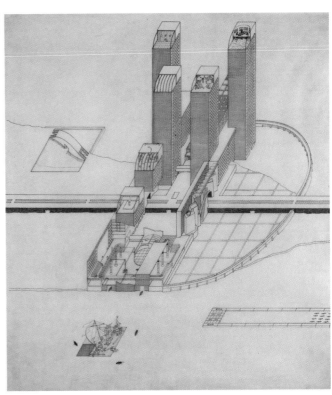

New Welfare Island
1975

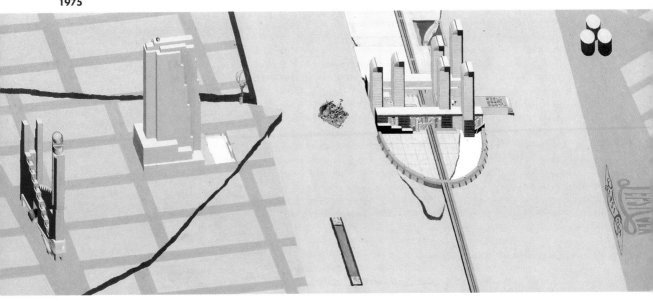

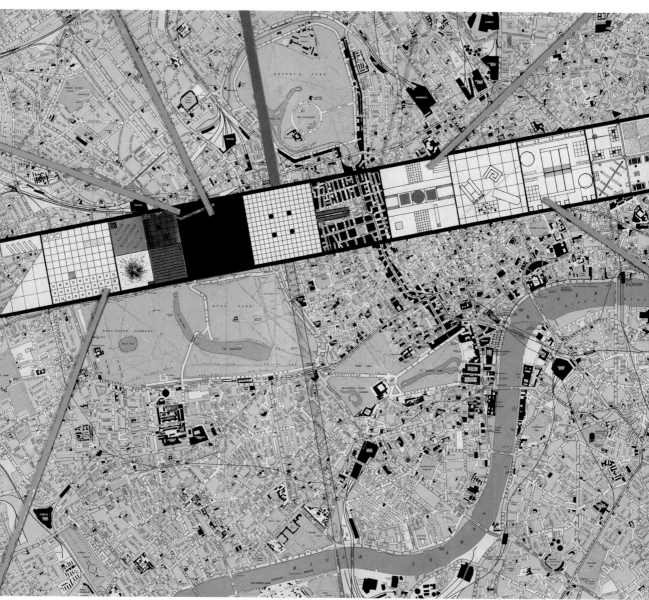

The Strip
1972

The Strip, aerial perspective
1972

concep
city

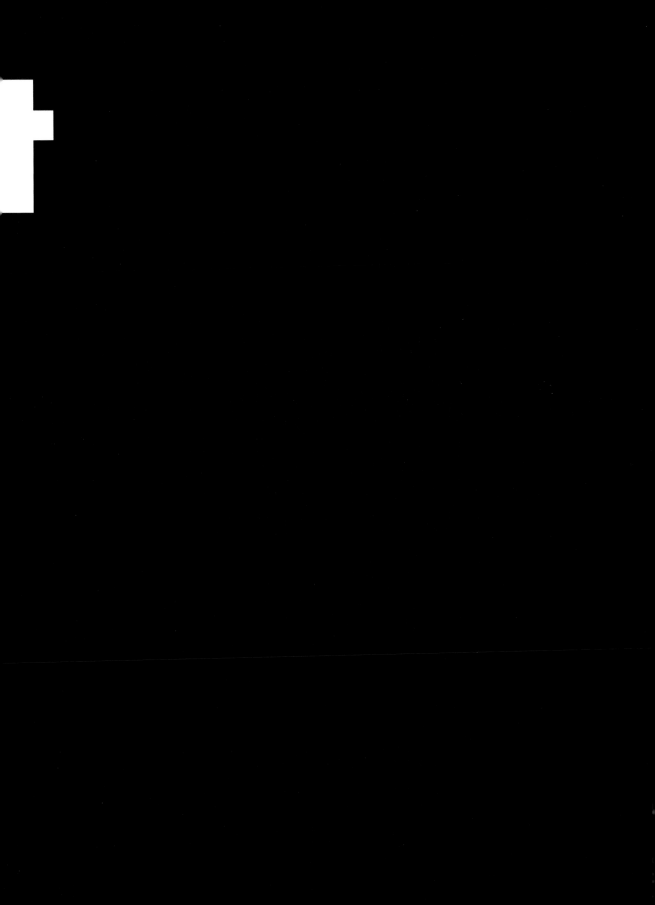

concept city

At the end of the 1960s artists began to occupy and work in urban space. In 1971–72, the Italian Gianni Pettena transformed a typical American suburban house into part of the natural landscape by covering it with ice and clay. In their work for the BEST Corporation, American architect and artist, James Wines and SITE created apparently incomplete facades and converted a parking lot into a monument by petrifying cars under a layer of asphalt. Another American, Gordon Matta-Clark, working in New York, advocated 'anarchitecture', a technique of subtracting rather than adding materials by taking parts from abandoned buildings. In Office Baroque, Antwerp (1977) Matta-Clark made semi-circular structural incisions in a dilapidated block due for demolition, creating a walk through 'panoramic arabesque.' Here architecture drew closer to conceptual art through concentrating on new methods of composing space, a deliberate rebellion against traditional guidelines. Later the New York based Diller + Scofidio again brought art into architecture with projects such as Slow House (1991) a meditation on 'vista' that explores the 'picture window' as the ultimate in advanced technology.

James Wines & SITE
BEST Indeterminate Façade
Houston, Texas, 1975 (concept by SITE)

Gianni Pettena

> 314

Ice House
Minneapolis, USA, 1971-72

Ice House II
1971

Ice House I
1971

James Wines & SITE

> 327

BEST Indeterminate Façade
Houston, Texas, 1975 (concept by SITE)

BEST

Canopy

BEST
sign

Canopy also
functions as
planting box

MOND SHOWROOM – BEST PRODUCTS

Wines
SITE

Richmond Showroom – BEST Products
1978

Homes

SITE GSSW-S
1981

Gordon Matta-Clark

> 307

Office Baroque
Antwerp, Belgium, 1977

Diller + Scofidio

> 285

The Slow House
Long Island, USA, 1991

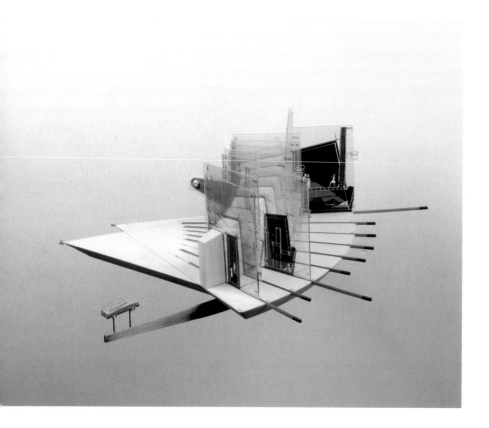

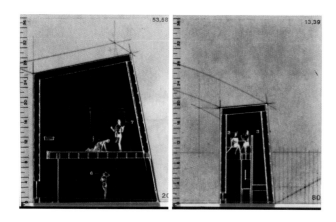

Didier Fiuza Faustino

> 288

1m2 House
2003

decons

ruction

deconstruction

Put simply, deconstructivist architecture disassembled and then reconstructed the elements of architecture such as columns, walls, roofs, stairs, windows and doors, so that new architectural techniques and structural freedoms could be developed. The 'Deconstructivist Architecture' exhibition held at the Museum of Modern Art in New York in 1988 helped crystallise its ideas. The exhibition highlighted the link between deconstructivism and the work of the French philosopher Jacques Derrida by presenting the projects and concepts of American and European architects such as Frank O Gehry, Rem Koolhaas, Peter Eisenman, Zaha Hadid, Bernard Tschumi and Daniel Libeskind.

A classic of the oeuvre, Open House (1983–92) by Coop Himmelb(l)au was designed by a method of unconscious drawing. Bernard Tschumi's grid-based Parc de la Villette project (1982–95) announced his concept of event architecture. An early regeneration proposal, Berlin City Edge (1987) by Daniel Libeskind is an exploration of how a city in crisis is transformed through an architecture imbued with memory. Later Lebbeus Woods, an American architect, used the aesthetic of shards to propose his High Houses (1994). These aerial houses did not have specific functional demarcations but allowed people to inhabit them as they wished. In Woods' philanthropic work the deconstructive aesthetic is turned away from affected nihilism towards a constructive end - as a balm with which to attempt to heal the ravages of Balkan civil war.

Bernard Tschumi
Parc de la Villette
1995

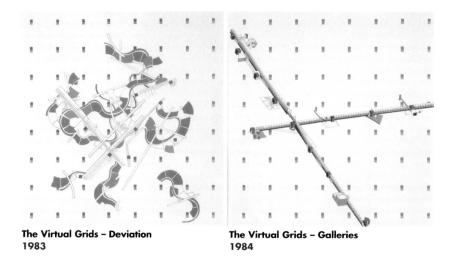

The Virtual Grids – Deviation
1983

The Virtual Grids – Galleries
1984

Parc de la Villette
Paris, 1982-95

Programmed Deconstruction
1983

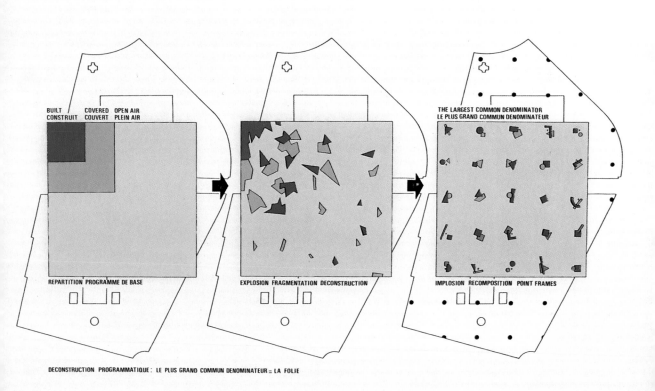

BUILT COVERED OPEN AIR
CONSTRUIT COUVERT PLEIN AIR

THE LARGEST COMMON DENOMINATOR
LE PLUS GRAND COMMUN DENOMINATEUR

REPARTITION PROGRAMME DE BASE

EXPLOSION FRAGMENTATION DECONSTRUCTION

IMPLOSION RECOMPOSITION POINT FRAMES

DECONSTRUCTION PROGRAMMATIQUE : LE PLUS GRAND COMMUN DENOMINATEUR = LA FOLIE

Bernard Tschumi

> 323

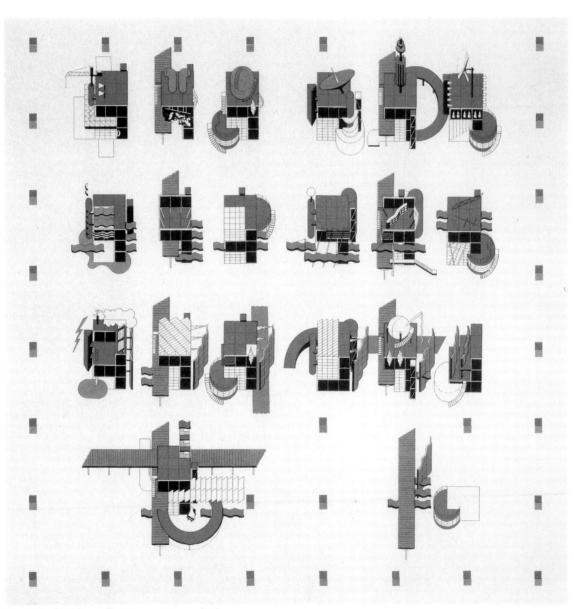

The Virtual Grids – Follies; Permutations of cube
1983

Submarine Folie
1992

Coop Himmelb(l)au

> 282

Project for Open House
Trancas Canyon, California, 1983–92

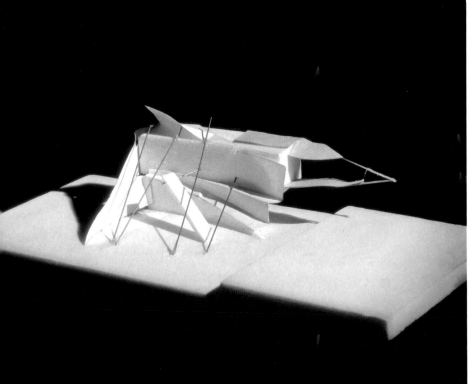

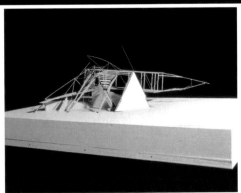

Peter Eisenman

> 286

Project for Guardiola House
Santa Maria del Mar, Spain, 1986–88

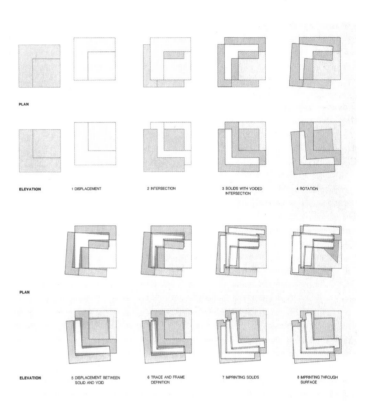

PLAN

ELEVATION   1 DISPLACEMENT   2 INTERSECTION   3 SOLIDS WITH VOIDED INTERSECTION   4 ROTATION

PLAN

ELEVATION   5 DISPLACEMENT BETWEEN SOLID AND VOID   6 TRACE AND FRAME DEFINITION   7 IMPRINTING SOLIDS   8 IMPRINTING THROUGH SURFACE

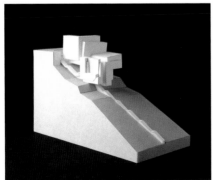

Massing Model

Structural Model

Daniel Libeskind

> 305

City Edge, Urban Competition
Berlin, 1987

Site Model B

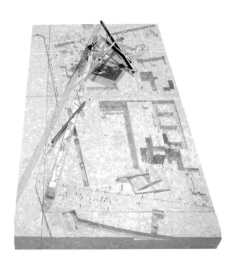

Site Model A

Morphosis

(Thom Mayne & Michael Rotondi)

> 308

Project for Malibu Beach House
Los Angeles, California, 1987

Eric Owen Moss

> 308

**Guest House
1991**

Michele Saee

> 318

Meivsahna House
Los Angeles, California, 1991

Asymptote

(Hani Rashid & Lise Anne Couture)

> 276

Steel Cloud
Project for Los Angeles West Coast Gateway
1988

Lebbeus Woods

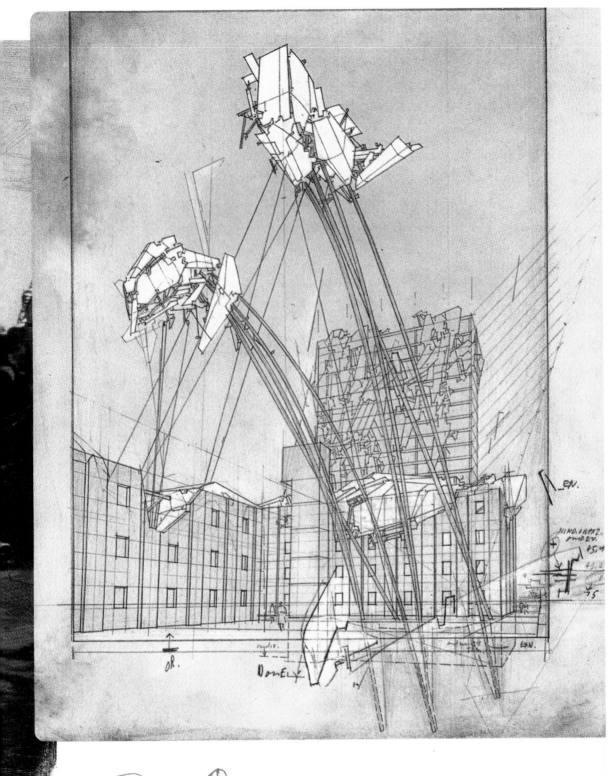

Zaha Hadid

> 294

The Hague Villas, the Hague Housing Festival
Netherlands, 1991

Spiral House
1991

Spiral House
1991

Spiral House
1991

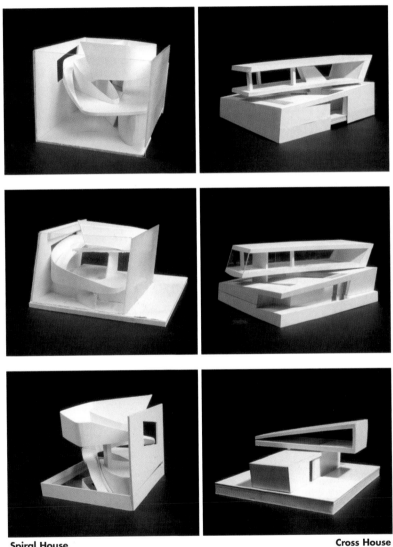

Spiral House
1991

Cross House
1991

Neil Denari

> 284

machine architecture

In the 1980s, the Californian architect Neil Denari became one of the main supporters of machine-like technological architecture. His proposal for the 1989 Tokyo International Forum Design Competition is considered to be one of the first architectural works of the information age. Also in America, Jones Partners Architecture (Wes Jones) used containers as minimum dwelling units, as part of a vehicular and mechanical architecture that created a link between the human body and technology. This machine-as-architecture has been made feasible by the development of digital techniques and new building materials.

**Tokyo International Forum Design Competition
1988–89 (Model 1988)**

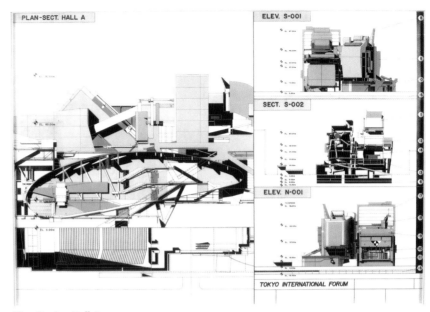

Plan Section Hall A

Plan Section E 001

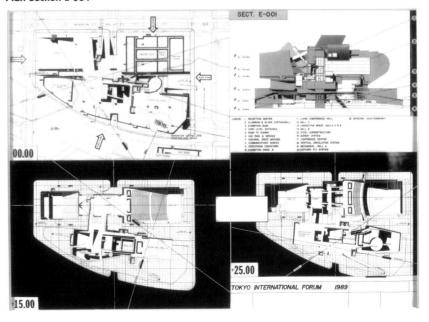

Jones, Partners: Architecture

(Wes Jones)

> 300

<blockquote style="float:right">Hesselink
Guest Hut
/ Container House</blockquote>

Front View

Primitive Hut Models
1998

urban
interve

ntion

urban intervention

During the 1980s London continued to be a focus for both inspiring teaching and of the production of architecture. Will Alsop and Nigel Coates are illuminating teachers and very able architects. Coates fostered his NATO group from students of his Architectural Association Unit. NATO (Narrative Architecture Today) embarked on what seemed to some outsiders as a determined effort to debunk all of the old established architectural tenets. To others they seemed to update and apply older ideas from the Situationists, Surrealists and Archigram to the contemporary city of London. London was the focus for much of NATO's work, the city's fecundity of consumer culture, post punk eclecticism, experimental urban living, and the beginning of hyperbranding were all grist to their mill. Later Coates was to update further the NATO vision with his Ecstacity (1992-2004).

Will Alsop, another alumni of 80s' eclecticism is now in his fourth decade of experimentation with an architecture that eschews normal taxonomy. It is vivid, often formally cacophonous, and uses material and colour in a most unconventional way. It take liberties with the city as a way to break it out of tried, tested and often tired spatial bondage and create catalytic urban moments.

Nigel Coates
(Detail) Gamma Tokyo
1985

NATO

> 280

Martin Benson
Albion from the Air
NATO No.1
1983

**Nigel Coates
ArkAlbion
NATO No.2
1984**

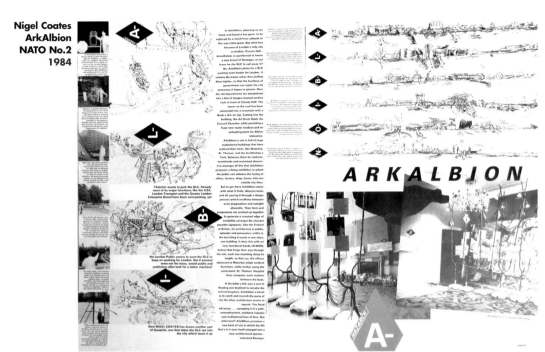

**Mark Prizeman &
Nigel Coates
Gamma Cities
NATO No. 3
1985**

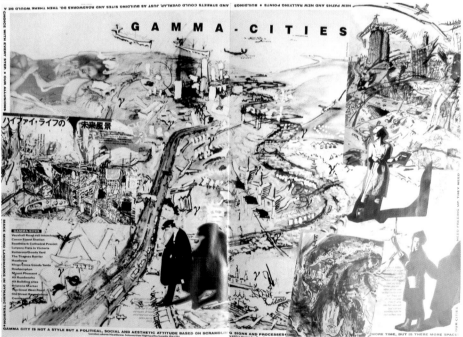

Nigel Coates

Ecstacity
1992–2004

Right. Aerial Hypologies
2000

Far right. Guide to Ecstacity
Designed by Why Not Associates
Published by Laurence King Publishing, London 2003

Map of Central Ecstacity
2000

Will Alsop

The Barnsley Project
2003

The Barnsley Halo
2003

experin
living

ental

experimental living

The house has always been a special subject for architects' experimentation. In many recent designs, the boundary between inside and outside has become an interactive space where borders between private and public are ambiguous. London based C.J. Lim + Studio 8 Architects have experimented by treating architecture as a cinematic production, erasing the boundary between building and environment. An example is their Guest House project (1995), where the building's appearance changes according to the climate and its inhabitants' lifestyle.

From the early 1980s, UK pioneers Future Systems proposed housing that took both its spatial and constructional inspiration from spacecraft, racing cars and yacht design. They created designs that had monocoque and semi-monocoque structures(common in aircraft design, particularly wings) that were transportable and adaptable. They have also developed an ecological emphasis as exemplified by their speculative Green Building (1990). More recently, Future Systems built what must be the most architecturally innovative shop in Britain. Their Birmingham Selfridges store reflects a signature approach; an urban intervention at once alien and sustainable, ergonomic yet spatially optimized and geometrically double curved.

Shigeru Ban has sought to revitalise the material palette of architecture, using inexpensive building materials such as paper logs and developing a pleasing translucent aesthetic at once relaxing and spatially complex. Log Houses have been utilised in situations of crisis to provide inexpensive shelter.

Eisaku Ushida & Kathryn Findlay also used this subtle Japanese aesthetic of translucency, but combined it with audacious curvilinear geometries and redesign the house typology with an astounding surreal quality that is both enclosing, sensual and functional. Their Truss Wall House (1990-93) and Soft and Hairy House (1992-93) are truly before their time and are an example of an aesthetic that many are still trying to mimic using computational technology.

Eisaku Ushida & Kathryn Findlay
Soft and Hairy House
1993

Future Systems

> 291

Blob
1985

Green Building
1990

Overleaf. Selfridges
Birmingham, 1999–2003

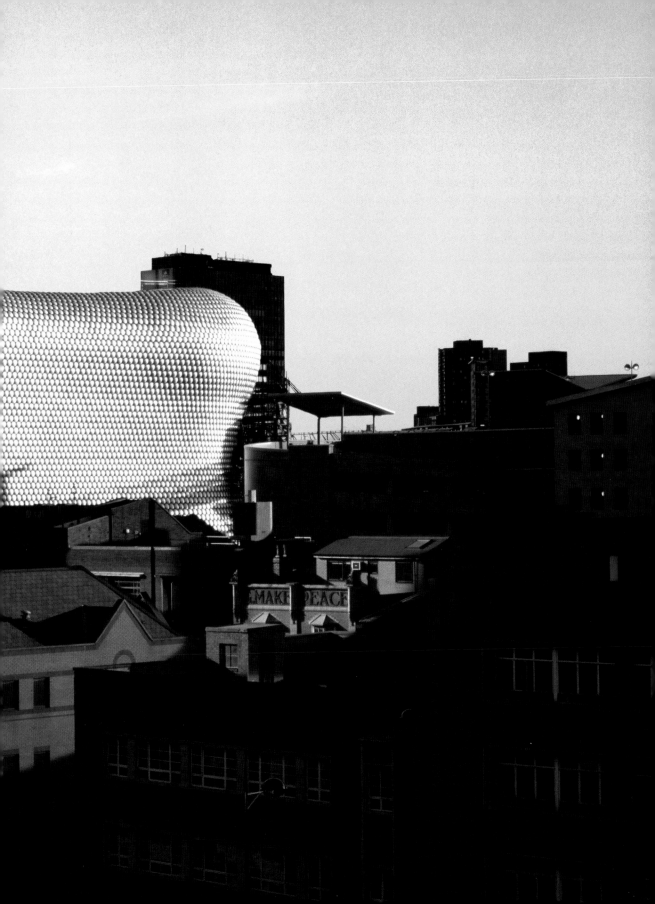

Eisaku Ushida & Kathryn Findlay

> 325

Truss Wall House
1990–93

Soft and Hairy House
1992–93

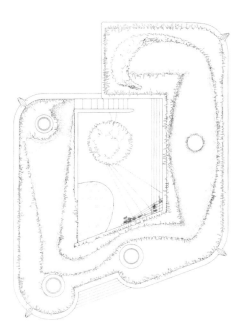

Paper Log House (Paper Tube Structure-07)
1995

Paper Church (Paper Tube Structure-08)
Kobe, Japan, 1995

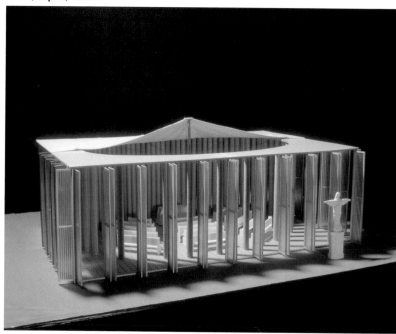

Paper Log House (Paper Tube Structure-07)
Kobe, Japan, 1995

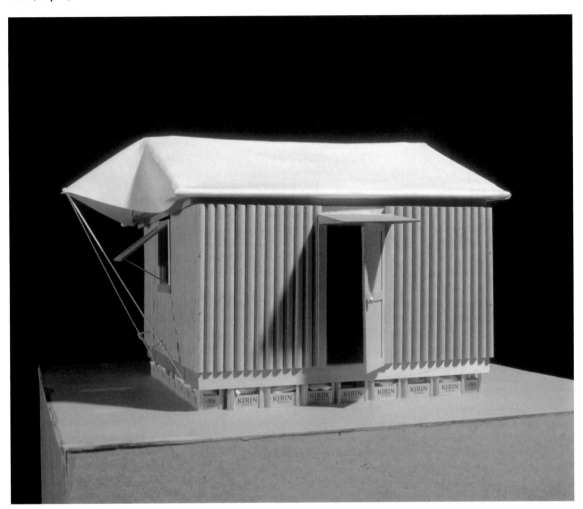

C.J. Lim + Studio 8 Architects

> 306

Project for the Guest House, the Landscape + Environmental Register
Japan, 1995

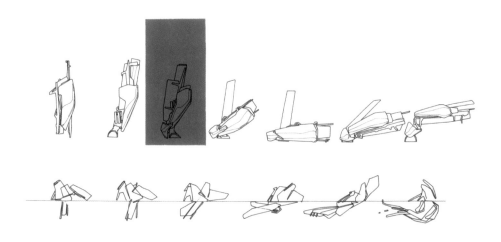

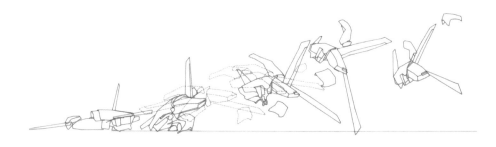

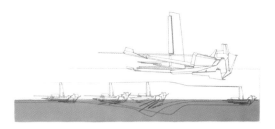

non-
standa
archite

rd
cture

non-standard architecture

During the early 1990s architects became seduced by the potential of cyberspace. Computer technology had advanced to the stage that urgent debates were held about whether it was possible to create a spatial architecture that would exist purely in the virtual world. As the 1990s progressed architects continued to experiment with this technology.

Nowadays computer-aided design is commonplace. A future is envisaged when architects will no longer be constrained by mass production and the limitations of standardised factory components. Forms that could only be dreamed about in the 1960s are now becoming realisable with the help of specialist software and computer driven machine tools advanced in the aerospace and car industries.

The envelope of NOX's Soft Office (2000) was to be created from a series of braided surfaces created on computer and, had it been built, machine instructions would have been sent straight to the factory.

In the project Resi-Rise (1999) Kol/Mac Studio used computers to blend the boundary between domestic appliances (baths, sinks and beds) to create a kind of seamless apartment interior, and to grow a whole apartment block. Some architects have attempted to construct elements of buildings that have the ability to respond to data streams in real time. dECOi's extraordinary Hyposurface, first shown at the Venice Biennale in 2000, is one such example. Others, such as Objectile and EZCT, have recognised that complex computationally drawn cutting and routing patterns can create minute landscapes and use them to create furniture and screens. As it now costs relatively little to fashion such ornate surfaces, decoration is part of the architectural debate once more.

Kol / Mac
Resi-Rise
1999

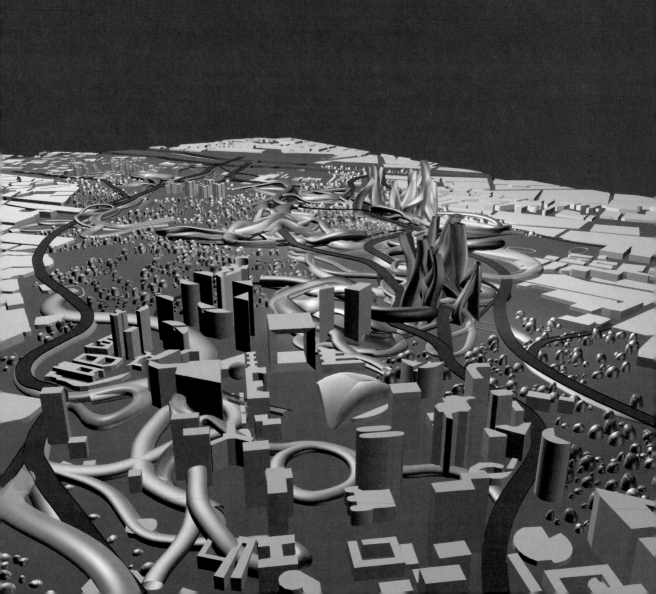

NOX

(Lars Spuybroek)

> 310

Soft Office
Warwickshire, UK, 2000

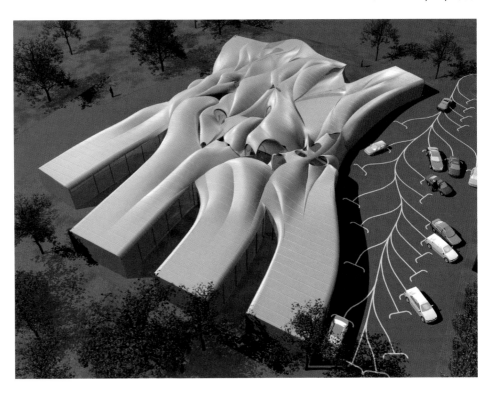

Left. ParisBRAIN
2001

dECOi

(Mark Goulthorpe)

> 283

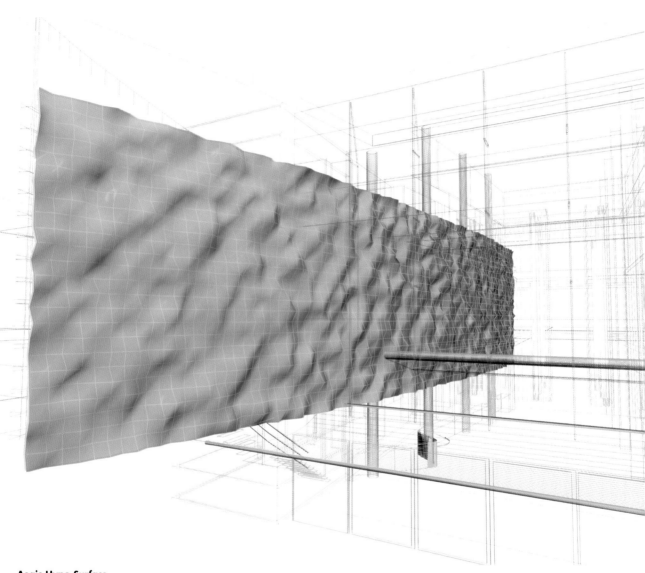

Aegis Hypo-Surface
1999

Aegis Hypo-Surface
2002

Kol/Mac Studio

(Sulan Kolatan & William Mac Donald)

> 302

Resi-Rise
1999

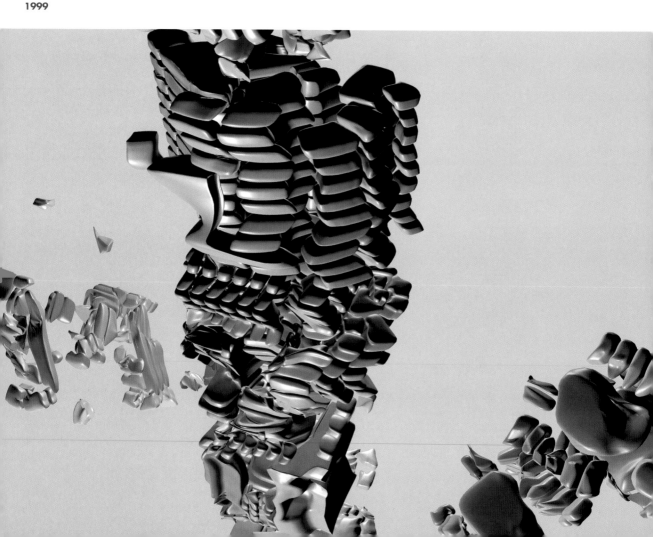

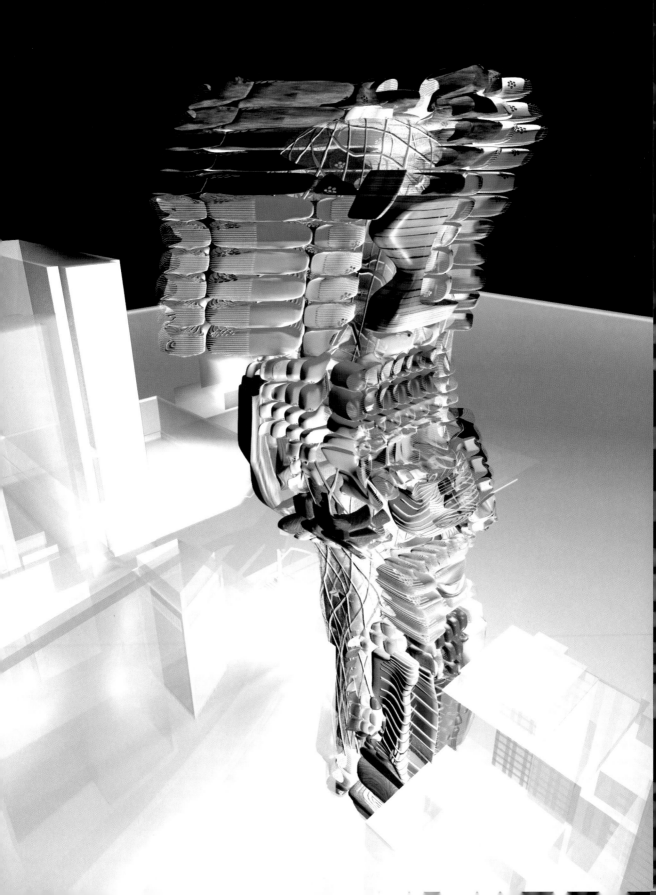

EZCT Architecture & Design Research

(Philippe Morel, Jelle Feringa, Felix Agid & Valerian Amalric)

> 288

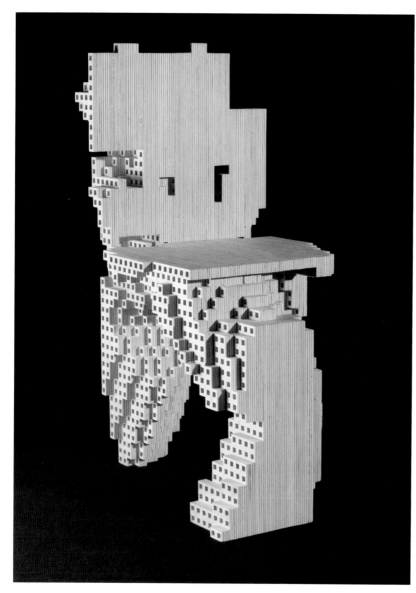

Studies on Optimization:
Computational Chair Design using
Genetic Algorithms (with Hatem
Hamda and Marc Schoenauer)
2004

Objectile

(Bernard Cache & Patrick Beaucé)

> 310

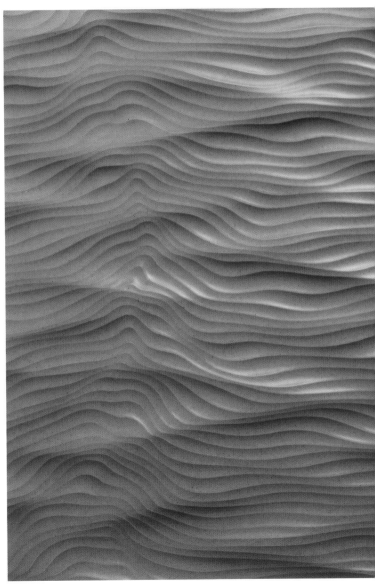

Panel
1998

Plateau of Table 'nymph'
1998

Untitled
1998

Périphériques

> 313

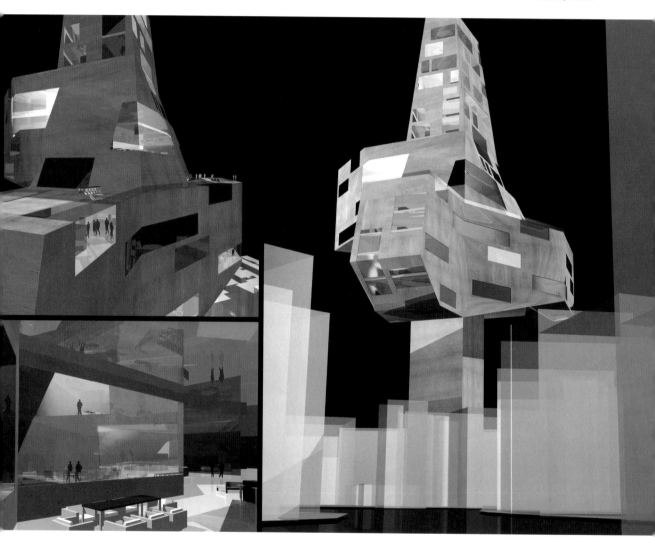

Tree Towers
China, 2004

Dagmar Richter Studio

(Dagmar Richter)

> 317

Project for the Wave, Gigantium Design Competition
Aarhus, Denmark, 2001

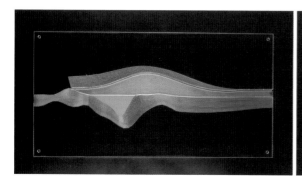 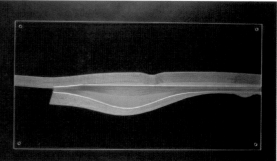

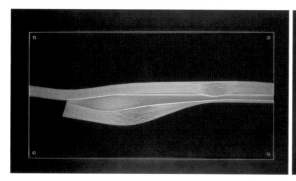 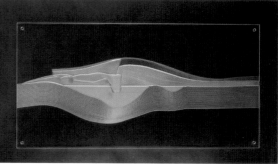

OCEAN NORTH

(Michael Hensel, Achim Menges & Birger Sevaldson)

> 311

World Centre for Human Concens
2001

contem

proces

porary

contemporary process

After the digital revolution, came a period where cyberspace, virtuality, biotechnology and even nanotechnology all have a potential impact on architecture and its future cities. We are still in the midst of this period.

Computation technology is a double-edged sword. It promises liberation from laborious work and instant, or near instant, communication. It promises smart interactive materials, surfaces and buildings. In the hands of skilled practitioners it allows for the creation of formal complexity and richness; some would say, even a completely new material paradigm. However, it can also lead to a culture of surveillance, 24 hour working and ecological damage. More evidently it can give rise to a ubiquitous curvilinearity and obsession with form making, seemingly at the expense of advancing social, ethical or radical ideas.

The task for current architects is to propose architectures that navigate and negotiate between these polarities and vicariously create future cities that are welcoming, enabling, facilitating, liberal and spatially exciting.

We live in an information society. All manner of data can be collected, transmitted and relocated, and this data can be used to create animated surfaces within a structure, while also forming the fundamental building blocks. Consequently the old typologies of architecture have become corrupted and blurred. Rem Koolhaas has made the transition from 'paper' architect to now being at the head of the OMA office. Their Jussieu Library (1992-95) and CCTV (1992-2008) projects are characterised by a utilisation of complex systems and circulation routes that conspire to form areas of easily navigable private spaces punctuated by areas of public access. Each building is a microcosm of the world city as a whole, familiar yet strangely alien, gratuitous yet rational.

MVRDV have become well known for the datascapes that literally shape the buildings they realise. Foreign Office Architects (FOA) analysed circulation flow to create the streamlined Yokohama Port Terminal (1995-2002).

Without the rapid evolution of the computer and its ways of processing and keeping check on large amounts of data, none of these projects would have been possible.

Foreign Office Architects
Yokohama International Port Terminal
Yokohama, Japan, 2002

OMA

(Rem Koolhaas, Ole Scheeren, Ellen van Loon, Joshua Prince-Ramus, Floris Alkemade, Reinier de Graaf & Victor van der Ghijs)

> 311

Concept Development Model

Overleaf. Partners in Charge: Ole Scheeren & Rem Koolhaas
CCTV Television Station and Headquarters
Beijing, China, 2002 (completion 2008)

Makoto Sei Watanabe

> 326

Jelly Fish 2 (LIQUID CRYSTAL) Soft Ice / Cold in the Balance
1994

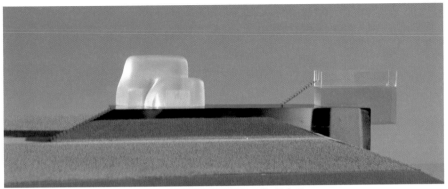

Jelly Fish 1
1990

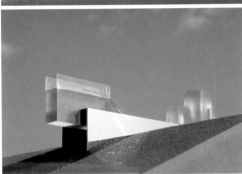

K-Museum
Ariake, Tokyo, 1994–96

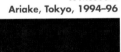

Foreign Office Architects

(Farshid Moussavi & Alejandro Zaera-Polo)

> 289

Yokohama International Port Terminal
Yokohama, Japan, 1995–2002

MVRDV

(Winy Maas, Jacob van Rijs & Nathalie de Vries)

> 309

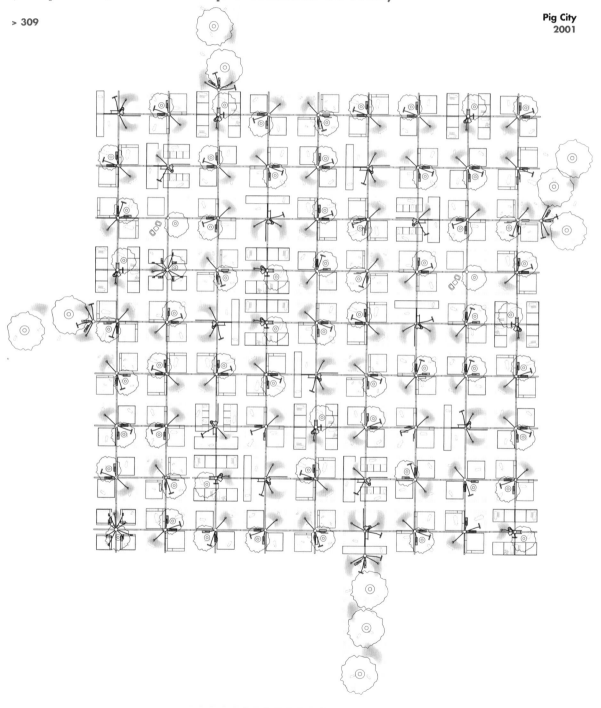

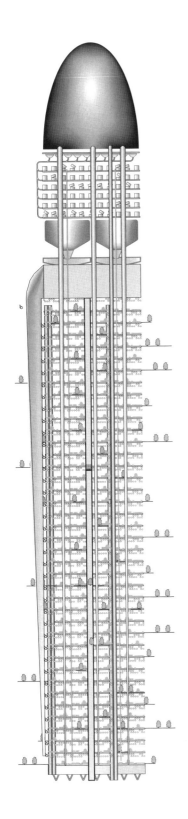

R&Sie...

(François Roche & Stephanie Lavaux)

(Un) Plug Building (Tour EDF)
La Défense, Paris 2001

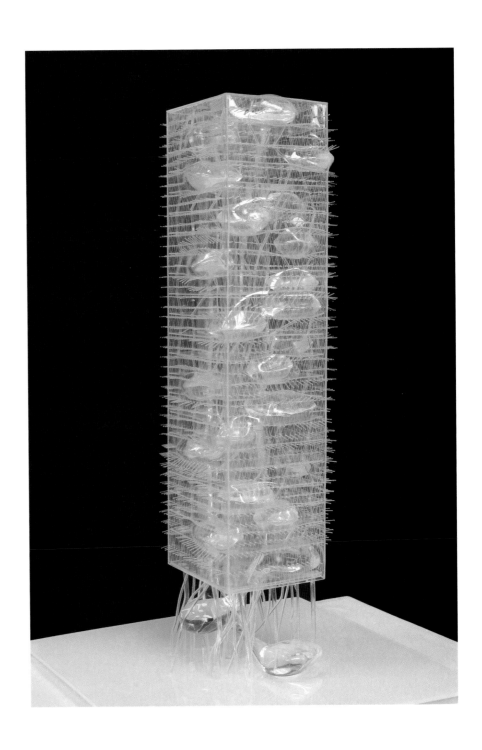

Silverelief / B-mu
Bangkok Contemporary Art Museum
Bangkok, 2002

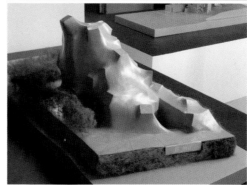

Jakob & MacFarlane

(Dominique Jakob & Brendan MacFarlane)

> 299

Docks of Paris, City of Mode and Design
2005–2007

Diller + Scofidio

(Elisabeth Diller & Ricardo Scofidio)

> 285

The Blur Building
2002

UN Studio

(Ben van Berkel & Caroline Bos)

> 324

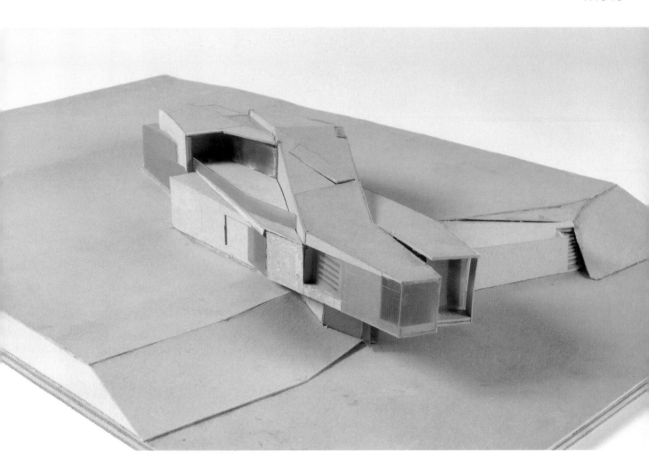

The Ziggurat, Mediatheque
New Orleans, USA, 2006

architects and works

architects and works

Will Alsop (1947)

Will Alsop was born in Northampton and studied at the Architectural Association in the 1960s. With fellow student John Lyall he established Alsop and Lyall in 1981. After the departure of Lyall and the arrival of Stormer, the practice became Alsop and Stormer in 1991. Alsop has been considered a maverick on the British architectural scene because of his striking avant-garde buildings. Apart from the £4.5 million Peckham Library (1991) his major commissions have come from mainland Europe, such as his government offices in Marseilles. Alsop works in an unorthodox way, putting his ideas into paintings first, and then gauging whether his creation can actually be built. He is seen as anti-modernist through his use of colour, bold shapes and his varied influences, from Pop art and music, to science fiction cinema and even comic books.

The Barnsley Project, proposal, 2003

Alsop's aim – in consultation with the people of Barnsley: professional architects, town planners, consultants, developers and the council itself is to re-make Barnsley, creating a true 21st century market town

This vision of a modern community that provides employment, culture, the arts, accommodation, leisure, retail and a place to relax, all focuses on its centre. Computer programs run by MIT demonstrate the medieval walled town, on which Alsop's designs are based, is the ideal model for a sustainable self-sufficient town. In this way Alsop is seeking to redress the modern malaise of towns bleeding away from their centres and becoming a collection of suburbs with no heart. However, instead of a defensive wall made up of ramparts, Alsop sees an inviting 'Living Wall' – a variety of structures complete with offices, shops and accommodation. This defines the limits of the town centre.

Inside the boundaries of this wall would be the modern equivalent of the medieval centre capable of supplying all its own needs in terms of power, food, economy and workforce. Easily accessed and welcoming gateways would attract people to the town. The town would be divided into districts: The Market, Courthouse, Church fields, each defined in function and purpose, providing an easily navigable and clear topography.

Architecture Principe
Claude Parent (1923), Paul Virilio (1932)

The meeting between Claude Parent and Paul Virilio in 1963 led to the formation of the Architecture Principe group, which espoused the exploration of the "oblique function", involving the conquest of the continuity of the sloping plane.

The partnership between Parent and Virilio would last five years, up until the upheavals of May 1968. Sainte-Bernadette-du-Banlay at Nevers (1966) represented the emergence of the very first radical application of this new theory. The two architects subsequently came up with a design for the Cultural Centre in Charleville (1967), which was never built. The same fate awaited the Mariotti House (1967), where the floor with its oblique surface did away with all obstacles, partition walls and stairways. The Thomson-Houston Centre, built at Vélizy-Villacoublay (1967–70), also complied with the 'oblique function', as did the house that Parent built in Neuilly (1974), and the Sens Supermarket (1970). So the oblique affected not only housing but also territorial and urban development. The bridge-structures duly became scalable and continuous, and the architecture became a means of moving about that offered 'liveable circulation'. Making the planes slope was thus an invitation to increase usable spaces by unfolding surfaces – a potential solution to the deep-seated concern with space-saving on the ground, so vital in our modern cities. The stairs then developed a different relation to the floor relieved of all obstacles, partitions and façades, where the furniture became a relief that was negotiable by being incorporated in the floor. The oblique gave the space back its fluid features required for free and enriching human relations, which are nowadays alienated or denied by the urban dwelling.

ARCHIZOOM Associati (1966–74)
Andrea Branzi (1938), Gilberto Corretti (1941),
Paolo Deganello (1940), Massimo Morozzi (1941),
Dario Bartolini (1943), Lucia Bartolini (1944)

With its name Archizoom, the Florentine firm founded in 1966 and dissolved in 1974, was paying homage to the English firm Archigram, while at the same time the onomatopoeic 'zoom', with its connotation of speed, conjured up the popular universe of comic books and Pop Art. Archizoom developed provocative furniture for Poltronova. Their pieces, the sofas Superonda (1966) and Safari (1967), for example, or the armchairs Mies (1969–70) and Aeo (Cassina, 1973), radically transformed the whole traditional approach to design. Even with their sometimes aggressive language (Safari, Dream Beds) and deliberate use of kitsch, these objects of design were presented more as a possibility for acting upon the real because they were intended to foster new behaviours in the user. However, with the Gazebi (1967–68), the Archizoom group embarked on an essentially theoretical path, their thinking directed more towards architecture's disciplinary and cultural role in its relationship to reality. Along with their experimental work in the field of design, the Archizoom group carried out research on cities, the environment and mass culture, which resulted in the project No-Stop City, an 'amoral' city without qualities, in which its citizens can assemble their habitat as a creative, free and personal undertaking; they can even design their own clothing (Dressing Design, 1971–73) as an urban experiment and an expression of their creativity. Finally, the members of Archizoom were, in 1973, among the founders of Global Tools, a counter-school of architecture and design, which supported the concept of the free development of individual creativity.

Letti di Sogno ('Dream Beds'), 1967
The authors of this project pass judgement on the civilization of the image. Dream Beds are 'micro-architectures', interior projects, which, in terms of design, offered an answer to the behavioural needs of a generation that could no longer tolerate

the constraints of the past. Archizoom wanted to introduce design from a critical perspective to the age of mass consumption. 'Neo-kitsch' objects, Dream Beds crossed references: an allusion to a 'new Empire style'; imitation marble in laminated plastic; a proliferation of symbols and signs in still more trivial references to the popular culture of the 1960s, steeped in Bob Dylan's music, or a psychedelic universe.

No-Stop City, 1969

No-Stop City is a critical utopia, a model of global urbanization, in which design is conceived of as a conceptual tool for modifying the quality of life and territory. The city presents the same organization as a factory or a supermarket. Interior spaces in No-Stop City, with air conditioning and artificial lighting, allow city-dwellers to organize new typologies of open and continuous habitation, intended for new forms of association and community. 'Considering architecture as an intermediate category of urban organization that had to surpassed, No-Stop City makes a direct link between the metropolis and furniture: the city becomes a succession of beds, tables, chairs and wardrobes, domestic and urban furniture meld into one. We respond to qualitative utopias with the only possible utopia: that of Quantity' (Andrea Branzi). Thus, No-Stop City infinitely extends its principle of the grid, absorbing furniture, architecture and city and providing everyone with an opportunity to recompose their habitat freely.

Asymptote
Hani Rashid (1958) & Lise Anne Couture (1959)

Hani Rashid (born in Cairo) and Lise Anne Couture (born in Montreal) founded their architectural firm Asymptote in New York in 1987. They think of architecture as a dynamic trajectory full of movement and speed. Practising an interdisciplinary approach that calls upon diverse specialists, their work puts forward a new fundamental architectural language open to new technologies. Engineering, telecommunications, speed and optical phenomena all contribute to a radically different and multidimensional understanding of space, 'architecture as the medium for an on-line experience', spatiality in constant mutation. Their project proposals include, therefore, not only buildings and urban projects but also multimedia installations and virtual digital environments that have been exhibited throughout the entire world. Whether it is their proposal for a Digital Transactions Room for the New York Stock Exchange, the Virtual Museum commissioned by the Guggenheim in New York, the Museum of Modern Art in Aarhus, Denmark or Fluxspace Projects, San Francisco, the responses to these programmes are based on disparity, liquidity, flow, mutation and the event. They recently saw completion of their project for the HydraPier, a building for art and technology in Haarlemmermeer near Amsterdam airport. Rashid and Couture also lead brilliant university careers across the globe. Professors at the Parsons School of Design and Columbia University in New York, they are also visiting professors at the University of Montreal, the Institut Berlage in Amsterdam and Harvard University

Los Angeles West Coast Gateway (Steel Cloud), California, unbuilt project, 1988

A gigantic aerial structure extending horizontally for almost 500 metres, this vast 'architectural anamorphosis' turns the idea of a void overhanging the motorway on its head; 8 metres off the ground, it is another city above the city. The cruciform structure of Steel Cloud is essentially composed of overlapping inclined planes, with no parallels. The functions envisaged for this enormous hanging piece comprise the

Museum of Immigration, two aquaria, gardens, a theatre, cinemas and a library. The concept of this architectural assemblage challenges any notion of scale. The two aquaria, like the hanging gardens, swing in the air, oscillating to the rhythms of the tides. A sculpture park literally detaches itself from the whole; the roof of the cinemas opens to offer a view of Hollywood; excerpts from the Genealogy Library are projected in different languages on huge screens that can be seen by drivers from the motorway. Using vocabulary similar to that of deconstruction, the architects took first prize in the competition, though the project was never built.

Shigeru Ban (1957)

Shigeru Ban, born in Tokyo, studied at the Southern California Institute of Architecture in Los Angeles (SCI-Arc) from 1978 to 1980 and then transferred to the Cooper Union School of Architecture in New York, graduating in 1984. He worked under Arata Isozaki for one year, then went on to establish his own firm, Shigeru Ban Architects, in Tokyo in 1985.

Ban has designed many buildings around the world, but he is most famous for his Paper Tube Structure Series. This series has included a wide range of designs, from chairs and temporary exhibition pavilions to houses and churches. He has produced temporary housing for use as emergency relief after the Kobe earthquake in 1995, the west Turkey earthquake in 1999 and the Bhuj earthquake in India in 2001. He also used cardboard tubes to produce refugee shelters to support the UNHCR (UN High Commissioner for Refugees) efforts in Rwanda. This emergency relief work attracted a great deal of media exposure. Later, in 2000, he worked in consultation with Frei Otto on the Japan Pavilion for Expo 2000 Hannover. He is also well known in France, particularly since ArchiLab 1999 in Orléans, and has become a worldwide celebrity. In 2003 he won the first prize in a competition for the new Metz Centre Pompidou in Metz, France, and is currently working on the design.

Always sensitive to the conditions of life in Japan's overpopulated cities, Ban's designs are open and pliant, and aim to construct spaces that are flexible. He reinterprets the methods used for traditional Japanese homes, aiming to maximize fluidity between internal and external spaces, and takes special measures to dematerialize a building. This makes it appear as though the space is spreading out towards the outside, liberating the house from the constraints of its walls.

Paper Tube Structure 1989–

Paper Arbor (1989) was Shigeru Ban's first work in the Paper Tube Structure Series that utilizes paper tubes as a structural material. Made from recycled paper, paper tube structures (PTS) had never been used as a structural material for constructing buildings, despite their advantages of being cheap, light and easily alterable to any length or diameter.

Ban thought that architects have a moral obligation to provide disaster victims with temporary housing and that doing so makes a small but significant contribution to the stability and well-being of society. Ban had used paper before, but his techniques progressed rapidly in the aftermath of the Kobe earthquake in 1995. The Paper Log House (Paper Tube Structure–07) produced at that time became the prototype for later temporary housing utilizing paper tubes. The log house looked warm and reassuring, providing 16 square metres of thermally insulated temporary living space (the paper tubes were waterproofed with clear polyurethane and, for Turkey, they were also stuffed with newspaper to enhance thermal insulation performance).

Paper Dome (Paper Tube Structure–09) is a frame structure with a 28-metre span. It is 8 metres high and covers a space 25 metres wide. To make the large span possible, wooden joints are used to connect straight paper tubes together instead of bending the tubes into shape. Composite panels are used as sheathing for the roof to provide rigidity. Light is let in through circular openings in the sheathing, and polycarbonate panels cover the whole structure.

Shigeru Ban has done away with the distinctions between temporary and permanent structures, creating original buildings by rethinking conventional construction techniques and methods instead of relying on new materials.

André Bloc (1896 –1966)

Painter, sculptor, engineer, architect and journal editor, André Bloc was an atypical and many-gifted creator who was at the centre of the French aesthetic debate after the war before he fell into obscurity after his death in 1966. Trained as an engineer and with a diploma from the Ecole Centrale in 1924, he was passionate about architecture and between 1925 and 1930 became an unreserved and committed Modernist. In 1930 André Bloc founded the journal *L'Architecture d'aujourd'hui*, which rapidly established itself as a forum for international debate about architecture. Subsequently he founded the art review magazine *Art d'aujourd'hui* (1949-54), which became simply *Aujourd'hui* in 1954. These publications became the vectors of a new form of cross-disciplinary thinking. In 1951, with the painter Félix del Marle, he founded the Espace group, which defended the principle of a synthesis of the arts, similar to that of Theo Van Doesburg and neo-plasticism in the 1920s, and in reaction against Le Corbusier. Between 1959 and 1962, Bloc worked on several chapel projects with Claude Parent, who helped realize Bloc's house at Cap d'Antibes on rocky terrain overlooking the Mediterranean (1959–64). From the 1960s André Bloc, working in his property at Meudon, executed some open-air sculptures – towers or labyrinths – as well as several 'sculptures-habitacles', reminiscent of the Demeures (dwellings) of Etienne-Martin. Using his own house as a subject, he studied the problem of integrating art into architecture: he defined the circulation spaces, designed the garden and conceived the polychrome interior and the furniture. In 1962, Bloc created Sculpture-Habitacle I in the garden of his property at Meudon. In 1996, thanks to the good offices of its commissioner, Frédéric Migayrou, the French pavilion at the VIth International Architecture Exhibition at the Venice Biennale paid tribute to Bloc, by way of an exhibition and a book entitled *Bloc: Le Monolithe fracture*, which represented the first opportunity since the 1960s to rediscover this complex creative figure.

Sculptures-Habitacles, Meudon, France, 1962-64

These sculptures in plaster, executed at Bloc's property at Meudon, date from his last creative period, around 1962–64. They reflect the research Bloc undertook using metal sculptures, which explored dimensional space, still influenced by the constructivism of the 1920s, by Gabo and Pevsner. The geometric configuration, which chipped the volume into ridges in the metal sculptures, here softened into an interior-exterior turning of space. The sculptures-habitacles may evoke troglodytic forms or primitive architecture, but they are above all a plastic experiment with space, which redefines the notion of habitat. Their perception of space is never front-on, but always involuted, so that there is no way of determining their anchorage. Built in several layers and pierced with holes, they define internal spaces of light and shade, like a hollowing out of fullness or an intensification of the limits of emptiness, appearing like open monoliths, with spatiality that is at once both connected and discontinuous. Neither expressionist nor brutalist or even formalist, the sculptures-habitacles of André Bloc must be read as a return to topological space which opens the plastic unity of forms to a spatial-temporal route, where the circumvolutions allow only the aesthetic form to be appreciated, projected between sculpture and architecture, being both modelled and architectural.

Chanéac (1931–1993)

Under his real name, Jean-Louis Rey, Chanéac began his initial research at Aix-les-Bains in 1958. This work would lead to what he referred to as 'industrialized–poeticized architecture', for which he filed a patent in 1969. A futuristic architect, Chanéac defended 'an organic, adaptable and mobile architecture', characterized by 'the free construction of individual cubicles', opening up a 'habitat for the greatest number'. Chanéac, convinced of the necessity of total industrialization, attempted to realize highly complex forms made possible by the use of plastic materials. In 1965, he joined the GIAP (Groupe Internationale d'Architecture Prospective), founded in Paris by the critic Michel Ragon. He was the winner of the 1969 Grand Prix International d'Urbanisme et d'Architecture in Cannes. From 1971, he participated in the 'Habitat évolutif' association with Pascal Häusermann and Antti Lovag. Chanéac went on to develop his concept of an 'insurrectional architecture', whose central premise was to foster end-users' involvement in creating their environment. He then designed the 'parasite cells', which, like suction cups, were designed to be affixed to the façades of major buildings. After Chanéac issued the manifesto of this theory in 1968, he and Marcel Lachat hung a renegade-bubble on the façade of a Geneva housing estate in 1970, which remained there for several weeks. Insurrectional architecture is founded on the idea of providing the individual with the technical resources required to create a personalized habitat. In 1971, Chanéac took part with Claude and Pascal Häusermann in the competition for the Paris Centre Georges Pompidou, for which he imagined a complex organic structure. In 1976, he built his own house in Aix-les-Bains, a complex organic form resembling an eye, staggered over several levels.

Polyvalent cells

Chanéac's 'polyvalent cells' (cellules polyvalentes; 1958–60) began his new reflection on modularity in architecture. These multipurpose shells could be juxtaposed and superimposed, until a neighbourhood or even an entire city was formed. In Savoy in 1962, Chanéac took just two hours to build an experimental dwelling composed of five factory-finished polyvalent cells. Mass production of these dwelling places reflected a vision of architecture as a response to a programme that is neither strict nor frozen. In 1966, Chanéac developed a prototype of a polyester cell (presented at ArchiLab in 2000 and 2003) with engineer Jean Nicoulaud. Chanéac described his polyvalent structures as 'biological cells proliferating in space responding to immediate needs as they arise with, as a counterpoint, entrenched megalithic structures'. These individual plastic cells rest on supporting spatial structures called 'space spiders' (*araignées d'espace*), adopting the form of a steel web to create a network. In 1963, he undertook his initial research on 'crater cities' (*villes-cratères*), seeking an answer to urban issues of the day. The crater city is an artificial landscape composed of 'canyons of circulation', corresponding to former streets dedicated to mechanical circulation, as well as 'artificial hills' and 'parasite cells'. Industrially produced and mobile, these 'cells' allow inhabitants of a city to change residential craters or supporting structures at will.

Nigel Coates (1949)

Trained at University of Nottingham and the Architectural Association, it is Coates' exuberant brand of design that has made him an international name in architecture. He was the first architect to articulate the concept of narrative, around which the experimental architecture group NATO was formed. His ideas come alive thanks to their wit and grounding in the real world. For him architecture is a form of communication and its language grows out of the whole matrix of city experiences. Throughout his career, Coates has pursued his ideas in exhibitions and publications amongst which his book, 'Guide to Ecstacity' (2003) is the most complete. He is Professor Architectural Design at the Royal College of Art, London.

Ecstacity, Painting1992 / Book 2003

Half-real and half-imaginary, the idea of Ecstacity builds on the increasingly global outlook of existing cities. It partners a fluid architecture of hybrids with the information world we already inhabit. It invests the everyday with the conflations of scale, of story, or emotion, replacing institutional power with shared grounds of identity and desire. In Coates' book, a summation of the project, each of the six sections frame an experiential interface with the city. They coincide to ask the question, 'What next for the city in the 21st century?'

Developed over a decade through various media, Ecstacity is a combination of the built and the unbuilt. It makes the case for a censorial and responsive architecture. It demonstrates how pluralism, and not uniformity, comes out of the multiplication of lifestyles and global communication. With scenes, streetscapes and buildings appropriated from Tokyo, Cairo, London, New York, Rome, Mumbai and Rio de Janeiro, Ecstacity constructs an urban kaleidoscope marked by cultural diversity and playful exuberance.

Constant Nieuwenhuys (1920-2005)

'We are becoming nomads', declared Constant in 1966. Co-founder of the CoBrA group of painters in the late 1940s, Constant dedicated himself as an artist, from 1956 to 1974, to New Babylon, the first project for a global city. Constant integrated the Bauhaus imagining into the search for an alternative to the Bauhaus and the CIAM (Congrès Internationaux d'Architecture Moderne), close to the dissident group Team X (founded in 1953), in which he developed his friendship with the architect Aldo van Eyck. From 1957 to 1960, Constant was a member of the Internationale Situationniste. In 1956, Guy Debord took up the themes of 'drift' and 'construction of situations'. New Babylon (1956–74) is thus the first global city marked by the 'planetary urbanism' of Guy Debord, who suggested its name. Characterized by disorientation, New Babylon is a 'dynamic labyrinth'. For Constant, mobility meant migration; the movement of individuals drives the transformation of architecture. In this, Constant perpetuates the precepts of 'shifting urban situations' held by Debord and the situationists, whose group he had definitively left by 1960. He also fell under the influence of megastructures, the 'streets in space' of Team X and Aldo van Eyck, who developed maze-like urban forms, as well as Alison and Peter Smithson in England, who were advocating 'incessant change' in the urban fabric and the complexity of 'human association'. In 1962, Constant, Friedman, Maymont, Frei Otto and Schulze-Fielitz all participated in the Amsterdam Mobile Architecture Exhibition. Most of the New Babylon models belong to the collection of the Gemeentemuseum in The Hague, where they were already on view in 1974. In 1998, the Witte de With art centre in Rotterdam held a retrospective of Constant's major works, assembling all of them for the first time since Constant decisively returned to painting after the end of New Babylon in 1974. Most recently, the documenta in Kassel held an important show of his work in 2002.

Peter Cook (1936)

In 1962, Peter Cook and David Greene launched the magazine Archigram, whose pop comic-strip appearance set it apart from other publications of the period. In 1963, the group of the same name was founded (Warren Chalk, 1927; Peter Cook, 1936; Dennis Crompton, 1935; David Greene, 1937; Ron Herron, 1930–1994; Michael Webb, 1937). Archigram was creating new architecture with the rise of consumer and leisure society: an architecture of communication nurtured by references to advertising, popular culture, the beginnings of computer technology and science fiction. Thought of as a service offering, architecture was to be consumed at the speed of images. The members of this informal association, which lasted until 1976, dispersed and mobile as they were, seldom had the opportunity to work on the same project all at once. The exhibition 'Living City' alone brought them together in 1963. It was a huge success and, like the writings of Reyner Banham, a friend and defender of the group, it helped ensure recognition of their work and spread their ideas. Presented as the group's spokesperson, Peter Cook participated in the group's main projects: Instant City with Ron Herron and Plug-in-City with Dennis Crompton. In parallel, Ron Herron designed Walking City; David Greene the Living-Pod; Warren Chalk Plug-in Capsule Homes; and Mike Webb The Cushicle. A professor at the Bartlett School in London, which he directed since 1990, Cook has also been professor and responsible for the architecture department at the Städelschule in Frankfurt since 1984. Winner of numerous prizes, Cook founded his own firm in 1975 in collaboration with Christine Hawley. Cook has also built housing in Berlin (Lutzowplatz Housing, 1993), Osaka and Frankfurt. In collaboration with Colin Fournier, he recently completed a building that has gained wide notice, the Kunsthaus (2003) in Graz, Austria, whose immense bubble, transparent or partially opaque 'skin' in acrylic sheets, thrusts upwards from the heart of the city like a huge floating vessel.

Instant City, 1968–69

A project for a nomadic city, on which Ron Herron also collaborated, Instant City consummates the disappearance of architecture, which has transformed into environment. Architecture gives way to the image, the event, the audiovisual, to gadgets and other environmental simulators. Instant City develops the idea of 'travelling metropolis', a package that temporarily settles down over the community. This city fleetingly superimposes new spaces for communication in the existing city: an audiovisual environment (words and images projected on suspended screens) and blends with mobile objects (dirigibles with hanging tents, capsules and mobile homes) and technological objects to create a city of information consumption, intended for a population in motion. The first stage of an information network, of education, leisure and facilities, Instant City transforms architecture into an event.

Coop Himmelb(l)au
Wolf Prix (1942), Helmut Swiczinsky (1945)

'Design architecture as floating and changeable as the clouds', Coop Himmelb(l)au declared in 1968. From the early 1960s, their radical action – architectural installations and happenings – took shape in urban spaces, as manifestos for an architecture of destruction, aggression, violence and death. The groundbreaking 1988 exhibition, 'Deconstructivist Architecture', at the MoMA in New York, thrust the Viennese group to the centre of the artistic and architectural scene. Their radical approach, between accident and the opening up of architecture to its own future, aimed to project basic emotions and sensations into space so as to achieve an 'open architecture' and create complex spatial situations, as variable 'as clouds'. A revealing example of Coop Himmelb(l)au's thinking on architecture, the Remodelling a Roof (1984–89) for a law firm in central Vienna opens and breaks its forms in the sky in a burst of flying glass. Regular participants in competitions, the firm won most notably the prize of the PA Award, given to them by the review *Progressive Architecture* in 1991 for the Open House. Their other best-known finished projects include the Funder Factory III in St. Veit-Glan, Austria (1988); the Video Clip Folly in Groningen, Netherlands (1989), construction of the studio of the painter Anselm Kiefer (1990), the Folly 6, a 27-metre observation tower for the 1990 Osaka Exposition (1990), the Rehak House, Malibu, California (1990), the Research Centre in Seibersdorf, Austria (1993–95), the Museum in Groningen, Netherlands (1993–94), the UFA Cinema Centre in Dresden (1998), the Habitation Tower in Vienna (2000) and Gasometer B, also in Vienna (1995–2000). The metaphor of the 'cloud' constantly reappears in the prestigious competitions they have won most recently, in the Musée des Confluences in Lyon (2005), the Client and Display Centre (Kunden- und Ausstellungszentrum) for BMW in Munich and the Akron Museum in Ohio, where the cloud can again be found floating in the air.

Villa Rosa, inflatable prototype, Vienna, 1968–69

Villa Rosa was a prototype for an inflatable, travelling habitat, displayed in different locations in Vienna. Composed of eight plastic bubbles, Villa Rosa recreated, at each presentation, a sensory space with which one could experiment. Its volumes could change shape, various sounds, colours and fragrances renewing one's perceptions at each location. Villa Rosa was both a purified space, a relaxation chamber, providing a décor for performances, and a wave of sensory experiences engaging the entire body. The architects proposed their ideas to NASA for use as psychic environments for astronauts.

Open House, Trancas Canyon, California, unbuilt project, 1983

The Open House project, an icon of the architecture of deconstruction, appeared on the cover of the 1984 catalogue *Architecture Is Now* (Rizzoli). The Open House displays the concept of 'open architecture' advocated by Coop Himmelb(l)au: '[O]pen architecture does not mean the house no longer has windows, doors or that it is transparent. For us, open architecture means an open mind.' Going back to the automatic writing of the surrealists, the house was designed with eyes closed, in a spontaneous process. The hand, like a seismograph, records and transcribes the feelings and emotions of the building, which in turn comes alive. Hence, building consists of conserving the energy of the original sketch. Façades and elevations, interior and exterior are thought out simultaneously and overlap like a series of X-ray photographs. From this are born highly visible phenomena of compression and dislocation shown in the small-scale model (identical to those in the drawing) and executed during the same phase of the work. The diverse stages of the development process retain the original elements of the initial sketch, whether conscious or unconscious, legible or inexplicable, and are a testimony to the fundamental place given to randomness as a programmatic issue.

Guy E. Debord (1931–1994)

In July 1957, the Internationale Situationniste was founded (it lasted until 1972), with Guy Debord its acting theoretician. The political activism of the IS was expressed, in part, through a different approach to the city: Guy Debord advocated at the time, with artist Constant Nieuwenhuys, the idea of a 'unitary urbanism' that 'envisaged the urban space as a playing field of participation' (IS, 1959). This game would take the form of urban 'drifting', inherited from the strolls of Thomas de Quincey in London or the 'promenade' of the surrealists, as in Le Paysan de Paris by Louis Aragon. 'The taste for drifting led to supporting all kinds of new types of labyrinth' (1958), which Constant's New Babylon plan would take into account, by imagining the 'planetary village'. This drifting would be inscribed in images by the collages of maps that Guy Debord made with the artist Asger Jorn.

Guide psychogéographique de Paris. Discours sur les passions de l'amour. Pentes psychogéographiques de la dérive et localisation d'unités d'ambiance, 1957. Editions Le Bauhaus Imaginiste, Copenhagen, Permild & Rosengreen.

Written in collaboration with A. Jorn, the Guide psychogéographique de Paris (1957) is indicated in Potlatch no. 29. The Guide breaks up the reigning unity of the plan to substitute urban 'unities of ambience', by subjective movements of the pedestrian, who recomposes his own urban space. Here, the itinerary of the bird's flight shapes the map. This collage of fragments of a Paris map, seen from a bird's-eye view, exposes the cut-out pieces of the map linked together with arrows indicating movement. For the conventional order imposed by the map and its implicit act of possessing the territory are substituted erratic wanderings, atmospheres and subjective disorder. The drifting, which signifies making oneself available to the different attractions of the terrain, to new encounters, refers to contingent time, to space reconstructed by the imagination, by experience – always fragmented and subjective.

dECOi (1991)
Mark Goulthorpe (1963)

In the architectural context of the early 1990s, marked as it was by the spreading philosophy of deconstruction, the firm dECOi (then comprising architects Zainie Zainul and Mark Goulthorpe) attracted attention as a result of several remarkable projects. These projects served as tools in their critical questioning of the validity of modernism. Mark Goulthorpe pointed dECOi towards research in digital information processing. Aegis (a vertical wall criss-crossed with waves that constantly modify its surface) – developed with engineer Mark Burry – questions the static logic of architecture by proposing to control form with information collected in real time. In these projects, Goulthorpe gradually came to define a new, more fluid and indeterminate logic of design that emphasizes the ability of digital technologies to improvise in the creative process, and which is expressed in form by the transition from the 'autoplastic' (totally determined relationship between the object and its environment) to the 'alloplastic' (permanent interaction). This guiding concept marked a significant break and led to the development of 'elastic' or parametric architecture. dECOi's projects often appear in a state of indecision, between form and non-form, solid and liquid, sculpture and interactive object. The idea is to incorporate the temporal dimension through the indeterminacy and evolution intrinsic to real-time information processing. To enable the seamless passage from computer simulation to a digitally manufactured prototype and then on to the finished object, the architect designed skins that are more flexible and interactive but which can truly be erected, such as the extension of the Dietrich House (London, 2000), the Folie of Excideuil (2001) or the Handelsman Flat (London, 2002). The transformation of the design process is thus intrinsically linked to that of industrial manufacturing.

Neil Denari (1957)

Through California architect Neil Denari, the architecture of the 1980s became fascinated with technology. His designs convey the coldness of all machines: neutrality outside all norms, objectivity and hyperrealism bordering on the surreal. Denari's output was best seen in publications. His two main monographs, *Interrupted Projections* and *Gyroscopic Horizons*, spread his projects like so many logos and icons. An exhibition of his work in the MA gallery in Tokyo in 1997 provided him with the space to set up his architectonic universe. Close follower of manufacturing processes invented by industry, Denari integrates new developments in materials and plastic. The Corrugated Duct House (1998) has an air-conditioning system that disappears between two metallic skins forming coffers and serving as cladding for the villa. Inevitably and justifiably compared with Wes Jones, whom he knew in his student days and who followed a parallel path, Denari stands out for the great importance he places on sleek surfaces. As Lebbeus Woods, another architectural visionary, observed, Denari is designing 'a world that is not the usual world of architects'. Since 1988, he has lived in Los Angeles and currently teaches at UCLA, after occupying the position as Dean of the SCI-Arc school from 1997 to 2000.

Tokyo International Forum, Japan, unbuilt project, 1989

Tokyo International Forum is the example of a successful attempt to establish a new dialectic between science and technology. Intended for a gigantic lot of 150,000m2, dominating the rest of the town, the spectacular size of this bright orange-coloured 'machine' appears in the urban landscape as an object of monstrous design, transgressing all relationship with scale. The Tokyo International Forum is a building one can cross from one end to the other, from the exhibition space to the theatre. Denari assimilated his readings of La Société du spectacle (The Entertainment Society) by Guy Debord, to define Tokyo as first and foremost a mental context, subject to urban and psychological compression. He also found inspiration in the films of Kurosawa to imagine this object, with its stretched surface resembling armour. The structure presents itself as technological envelope, and, like Tokyo, an envelope of communications transactions aiming for technological domination in the world economy. This architect considers the world of technology and architecture as part of a culture of effects and environments more than as defined form.

Diller + Scofidio
Elisabeth Diller (1954) & Ricardo Scofidio (1935)

Since 1979, these two American architects have shown their work internationally in exhibitions, set designs and theatrical performances. In their approach, they explore the interferences between architecture and other cultural systems – film, fashion, philosophy, theatre, plastic arts and media arts. They also adopt their own narrative form in their work, by integrating texts in their installations, combining several levels of understanding like a 'hypertext' or developing a scenario inside of an architectural or visual arrangement. For Diller + Scofidio, all technological transformation is tantamount to creation of a new system. In all their projects, reality becomes hazy or, rather, our certainties about its definition become so. In Master/Slave, an installation shown at the Fondation Cartier in Paris, they put robots on stage, human simulacra transformed by the intermediary of screens, mirroring for the spectators their own position as simulacra of machines. Their recent creation, which attracted great media attention was the Nuage for Expo 02, on the lakeshore at Neuchâtel, Switzerland, named Blur Building. Speaking about this, Elisabeth Diller insists that 'there was nothing to show, other than perhaps our dependence on sight'. They also produced the Slither Housing in Gifu, Japan, in 2000, a collective housing project that appears as a vast serpentine line of approximately 100 housing units, providing a unique walking experience.

Elizabeth Diller attended the Cooper Union School of Art and received a Bachelor of Architecture degree in 1979. She then taught at the Cooper Union and has been Associate Professor of Architecture at Princeton since 1990. Ricardo Scofidio also studied at the Cooper School of Art and in 1960 received a Bachelor degree in Architecture from Columbia University. He has been professor of architecture at the Cooper Union School since 1965.

Diller + Scofidio was formed in 1979. They have received the Macarthur Fellows program as well as the Macdermott award for creative achievement from MIT and the Tiffany award for emerging artists.

Slow House, Long Island, NY, unbuilt project, 1991

The Slow House was designed for an approximately 1-hectare site on Long Island. It won the 1991 award from the review *Progressive Architecture* in New York, and has since been discussed many times over in art and architecture reviews. The house spreads out in a vision of a conical form, gradually widening as it approaches the sea. The Slow House draws its inspiration from the film *Le Mépris* shot at the Villa Malaparte on the island of Capri by the director Jean-Luc Godard. Visitors leave their cars and enter through a door the size of a façade. The undivided interior space leads in one long sweep from the door to the window overlooking the sea. The occupant is thus 'visitor', who crosses the empty core of the architecture. Inside, a television broadcasts images of a landscape, in real time or not, offering a retroactive view. One's perception here tends to be drawn towards the fictional mode of television, film and their surveillance systems. The space for vision broadens to include the cultural and political space of the media.

Blur Building, built, 2002

Described by *Architecture Magazine* as 'an inhabitable cloud whirling above a lake,' the Blur Building was designed as a media pavilion for Swiss Expo 2002, constructed on Lake Neuchâtel in Yverdon-les-Bains, Switzerland.

Approached via ramps and walkways and constructed from piles in the water and a system of struts and rods, the form is reminiscent of the work of Buckminster Fuller. The Pavilion is made of filtered lake water shot as fine mist through 12,000 fog nozzles creating an artificial cloud 300 feet wide by 200 feet deep and 65 feet high. An inbuilt weather station controls fog output in response to shifting climatic conditions.

From the bridge, visitors walk onto a large open air platform in the centre of the fog mass. Once inside the fog there is an optical 'white out' and only the 'white noise' of pulsing water nozzles. Before entering the cloud each visitor responds to a questionnaire/character profile and receives a 'braincoat' (smart raincoat). The coat is used as protection from the wet environment and storage of the personality data for communication with the cloud's computer network. Using tracking and location technologies, each visitor's position can be identified and their character profiles compared to those of any other visitor.

Inside the Glass Box, a space surrounded by glass on six sides, visitors will experience a 'sense of physical suspension only heightened by an occasional opening in the fog.' As visitors pass one another their coats will compare profiles and change colour indicating the various degree of attraction or repulsion, much like an involuntary blush: red for affinity, green for antipathy. The system allows interaction among 400 visitors at any time.

Visitors can climb to another level to the Angel Bar at the summit. The final ascent resembles the sensation of flight as one pierces the cloud layer to the open sky. Here visitors relax, take in the view, and choose from a large selection of commercial waters, municipal waters from world capitals, and glacial waters. At night, the fog will function as a dynamic and thick video screen.

Peter Eisenman (1932)

By 1988 and the time of the exhibition on 'Deconstructivist Architecture' on the ideas of the philosopher Jacques Derrida, organized at the MoMA in New York by Mark Wigley, Peter Eisenman already had a long career behind him as a teacher and theoretician. A member of the group known as the New York Five, he developed research that was radically conceptual, notably through an experimental series of 13 individual houses – of which five were actually built. He designed these dwellings based in purely formal transformations using a minimalist approach close to that of Sol LeWitt or Donald Judd. A major figure in deconstructivism, Peter Eisenman has written many theoretical works and taught in American and European universities. He received a prize in 1991 for the Koizumi Sangyo Corporation Headquarters in Tokyo (1990) and in 1993 for the Wexner Center at Ohio State University in Columbus (1989). His extremely prolific production includes works such as the Greater Columbus Convention Center, Columbus, Ohio (1989–93) and the Aronoff Center for Design and Art at the University of Cincinnati (1988–96). In his latest projects, greater use of the computer led Eisenman even further into the realm of formal and even more complex manipulations. All of Eisenman's projects begin with a relationship to a written philosophy and understand architecture as a structure for process. Deeply affected by the events of the Shoah and Hiroshima, Eisenman questions the supremacy attributed by the West to human values. The architect seeks to decentre the human subject, to reintroduce disorder and instability. Making use of various notions such as grafting, the trace, the imprint, superimposing, the Möbius strip, the structure of DNA or the building to scale of ever more complex projects, Eisenman strives to bend the relationship of dominance of the mind and the eye in architecture, seeking to dislocate vision, thought and subject.

Guardiola House, 1986–88

The Guardiola House is emblematic of Eisenman's analytical approach, imbued with linguistics, philosophy and psychoanalysis. At the time the philosopher Jacques Derrida was working on the text about the Chora in Plato's *Timeus*, Eisenman began to design the Guardiola House. In parallel, these two men collaborated on the garden Chora L Works – never built – for the Parc de la Villette in Paris. Both projects attempt to represent the idea of the chora, or receptacle of forms defined by Plato as a non-place, situated between container and content. Antecedent of all that exists, the chora by definition cannot be represented: it is neither object nor place. It follows the movement of shapes, which leave a trace, and acts as a sort of 'imprint-holder' of sensitive creatures. Eisenman superimposes on to Derrida's his own notion of imprint and trace, of which the Guardiola House is the embodiment – an idea of the foot leaving its imprint in the sand and the trace of the sand on the foot in this reciprocal movement between impression and tracing, presence and absence. The Guardiola House results, then, from the operations of shifting and superimposing a basic geometric figure, the cube, and evokes, as would a wave on the sand, the trace left by the decomposition of this volume's slippage as it slides down a slope. It manifests, as do the other houses of the series begun in 1967, this quest for architecture for architecture's sake, which refers only to its own characteristics and which has no other signification than processes that generated it.

David Georges Emmerich (1925–96)

Originally from Hungary, David Georges Emmerich was deported during the war. He arrived in France in 1953, where he completed his education at the Paris Ecole des Beaux-Arts. In 1956, he participated in the Xth International Congress of Modern Architecture (CIAM) in Dubrovnik. Faced with the general lack of comprehension regarding the research undertaken by these architects, Yona Friedman created the GEAM (Mobile Architecture Research Group) in 1957 in Paris. Emmerich's work echoed the ideas of this organization. He began regularly registering patents to protect his inventions based on the principle of self-tensile structures. During the 1960s and 1970s, he published several articles in architectural reviews. Emmerich dedicated his entire life to research on the morphology of structures and to teaching about new methods of construction. In France he was the greatest defender of structural research in architecture, on a par with other major figures like Robert Le Ricolais and, from the 1930s, Konrad Wachsmann, Z.S. Makowski and R. Buckminster Fuller. These architect–engineers were developing the notion of spatial or three-dimensional structure, which was designed to lighten mass. The concept of 'spatial grid' opens a hybrid space where the elements of stress and compression are evenly distributed through the articulation of identical modular elements. The techniques for assembly Emmerich advocated were intended to facilitate the development of self-construction and thereby confer on each individual the right to build in an affordable and democratic system.

Self-tensile structures

At the end of 1958, Emmerich conceived the principle of tensile structures based on the game of jack-straws, where the balance between traction and compression results in a stable and stress-resistant construction. This system of small chains and sticks constitutes the chords and rods that define a polyhedral configuration in which all the elements reinforce each other. In this sense, self-tensile structures are modular systems or building kits. Combinations of these structures were expected to enable construction of convertible dwellings with organic growth, multiple uses and without separations, characterized by the lightening of their mass and the flexibility of their elements.

EZCT Architecture & Design Research
Philippe Morel (1973), Jelle Feringa (1978),
Felix Agid (1979), Valerian Amalric (1975)

Founded in 1999, EZCT are conducting architectural research on the rapid interpenetration of the sciences and technology (*Architecture as Sport, Werk, Bauen + Wohnen*, 2002; *Convergence Technologique*, lecture IFA, 2003) through their association with theorists and university academics coming from their various fields of discipline. The synoptic vision of architecture this enables is not only cultural or artistic but epistemological as well. The firm is currently working on the relationship between calculus and architecture (*Quelques précisions sur l'architecture et les mathématiques, Rencontres Mathematica® IHP*, 2004. *Notes on Computational Architecture*, Virtualmediacentre, online, 2004; EZCT places great importance on creation defended with new concepts: integral capitalism, neuromarketing (*From Neuroscience to Neuromarketing, Radical Shifts in Marketing & Communication Strategy*, 2003) and biocapitalism *(Research on the Biocapitalist Landscape*, 2003). Equally important for them are precise analyses of reality, removed, however, from all forms of stylistic realism. In 2003, EZCT participated in the workshops held at the architecture school Paris–Malaquais and the Technical University of Delft, Netherlands. They collaborated in designing the scenography for 'Architectures non standard' at the Pompidou Centre (2003) – work they presented at the International Mathematica Symposium 2004, Banff, Canada – and participated in Performative Architecture at the Technical University of Delft. EZCT's most recent work is *Empirisme et objectivité, investigations architecturales avec Mathematica* (2004).

Studies on Optimization: Computational Chair Design using Genetic Algorithms (with Hatem Hamda and Marc Schoenauer) 2005
EZCT have created a revolutionary way of designing a chair based on the theories of Charles Darwin. Approaching the Platonic ideal of a true chair in a scientific way, EZCT aim to find a synthesis of evolutionary science and mathematics.

Didier Fiuza Faustino (1968)

Didier Faustino uses the body to try and breathe life into space. His obsession with this renders his artistic and architectural productions indissociable, though they should in theory be distinct. He has thus been able to experiment with and probe the fields of perception to test the body's limits. Which is it, the body or the architecture, that is being manipulated? In Alice's House, the latex crack overwhelms the two linked pavilions, offering an unstable access to inhabitants and rendering them inescapably aware of their corporal nature. Personal Billboard: an Urban Peep Show features a house in which the only window is a giant screen upon which the user can project images that may represent reality or fiction – who is to say which? More than a simple steel chair, Love Me Tender, the interface between architecture and the individual, provokes discomfort and unease, but the 'victim' here is the architecture, as with every movement the chair claws its surroundings with its sharp points. Faustino likes to work with what he calls the 'basic elements' of architecture to upset preconceived ideas. His projects, such as Body in Transit (2000, coll. Pompidou Centre), a case for transporting clandestine passengers by air in a sort of minimum habitat, sharply highlight social and political issues. They inspire doubt and place the inhabitant in a danger zone. Faustino has been in practice since 2001 with Pascal Mazoyer in the firm Bureau des Mesarchitectures, which earned them an entry in the Albums de l'architecture 2002 in France.

One Square Metre House, proposal, 2003

'An ideal place to rest after days spent in public engagements and nights in clubs. Your own house, available now in a wide price-range: between two and five floors on a one-square-metre site, for the price of the plot of land. Choose your level of luxury. Incredible! It's so affordable that you can at last have a house wherever you go.' Thus sets out architect Didier Fiuza Faustino the merits of his One Square Meter House, a response to the urban overpopulation of our modern lifestyle. The One Square Meter House is, however, a 'mini-nightmare' as well as a neo-Metabolist vision of the dwelling of the future: it achieves an overall height of 17 metres – some five or six storeys – by superimposing standardized translucent resin shells linked by a metal ladder. Thus the house is both cramped and exhausting (you have to climb up 17 metres to reach the sleeping level, which is only big enough for a single person of medium size), and it expresses the worst qualities of individuals (determination to own property at all costs, exhibitionism and egocentricity).

Foreign Office Architects (1995)
Farshid Moussavi (1965) & Alejandro Zaera-Polo (1963)

Foreign Office Architects (FOA) was set up by husband-and-wife team, Zaera-Polo and Moussavi in 1995. Zaera-Polo studied architecture at the ETS of Architecture in Madrid, while Moussavi was a student at the University of Dundee and the Bartlett School of Architecture. Both studied for Masters at Harvard Design School (where they met) before a spell working with Rem Koolhaas.

They see teaching as an important part of their work and this continues at the Architectural Association, as well as the Harvard Graduate School of Design, Princeton and Columbia Universities in the United States. FOA embrace diverse lines of research including explorations into process, landscape, typology, ornamentation and iconography. FOA believes in an architecture rooted in life and take pride in a capacity to work creatively with the particularities and constraints of any given project.

Yokohama International Port Terminal, Japan, built, 2002

The project brief was to combine a passenger cruise terminal with a mix of civic facilities for the use of citizens in one building. The site has a pivotal role along the city's waterfront. If declared a public space it would give the city a continuous structure of open public spaces along the waterfront.

The FOA proposal shows the roof of the building as an open plaza, continuous with the surface of Yamashita Park as well as that of Akaranega Park. The project starts with what the architects have named the 'no-return pier', structuring the precinct of the pier as a fluid, uninterrupted and multi-directional space rather than a gateway of fixed orientation. A series of interlocking circulation loops allow the architects to subvert the linear and branching structure characteristic of such a building.

The building is seen as an extension of the urban ground, constructed as a systematic transformation of the lines of the circulation diagram into a folded and bifurcated surface. These folds produce covered surfaces where the different parts of the civic programme can be hosted. The relation between the skin and the areas established by the structural folds of the surface is one of the most important aspects of the project: the folded ground distributes the loads through the surfaces themselves, moving them diagonally to the ground. This structure is also especially adequate in coping with the lateral forces generated by seismic movements that affect the Japanese topography.

Bundled Towers WTC, proposal, 2002

As high-rise buildings become taller, the strength of the material that acts as structure starts to become more susceptible to bending. So until recently the only solution was to keep increasing the depth of the floor plans. This leads to building whose floors are extremely deep and therefore heavily reliant on artificial ventilation, artificial lighting and do not afford many occupants with a view of the outside. Often tall buildings such as the previous World Trade Centre or the Petrona Towers are divided into pairs of matching towers to avoid the deep floor plate problem as much as possible.

FOA's proposal for the World Trade Centre site after 9/11 was to think of their building as a series of bundled interconnecting towers that provide flexible floor plates and structurally buttress each other. This concept works microcosmically as the structural columns twist in space buttressing one another but also spatially as each tower supports each of the others.

This new high-rise structural topology is enabled by the use of computers, as it would often be impossible to do all the interrelated structural calculations by hand. Computers allow architects and engineers to visualise the stresses and strains graphically, which enables them to see zones of likely collapse and mitigate them, whilst the proposal is still simply a computer model. The continued exponential development in software and hardware is having a huge impact on the sort of structures that we can conceive of and build. Complex double curved surfaces are fashionable because architects have been starved of the possibility of such structures for centuries.

Yona Friedman (1923)

Born in Budapest, Yona Friedman studied there before pursuing further training at the Technion in Haifa, Israel. Already in 1954 Friedman attempted, with the inhabitants of Haifa, an initial experiment in housing designed by its future inhabitants. In 1956, at the Xth International Congress of Modern Architecture (CIAM) in Dubrovnik, Modernism was subjected to intense questioning. For the first time, Friedman developed his ideas about the principles of architecture that could foster 'social mobility' thanks to habitats and urban structures that could be transformed by inhabitants. In 1957 he settled permanently in Paris, where he founded the GEAM (Mobile Architecture Research Group). In 1958 he set out the principle applied to the 'spatial city', i.e. a three-dimensional structure. His research began to inspire the visionary projects of Archigram in London around 1963 and the Japanese Metabolists during the 1960s and 1970s. Around the mid-1970s, Friedman was preoccupied with designing dwellings for developing countries in Asia, Africa and South America. In 1987 he completed the Museum of Simple Technology in Madras (now Chennai), India, a project that implemented the principles of do-it-yourself constructions using locally available materials such as bamboo. His international standing puts Yona Friedman in great demand and he lectures tirelessly all over the world.

Spatial City, 1958–60

In 1958, Yona Friedman published his first manifesto, Mobile Architecture. The mobility in question is not that of the building, but rather its users', to whom the granting of new freedoms is envisaged. The term 'mobile architecture' means, therefore, the 'habitat decided by the inhabitant' through 'non-determined and non-determinant infrastructures'.

In the spatial city, constructions must:

1) 'Touch the ground, occupying a minimum surface area
2) Be easily broken down and moved
3) Be transformable at will by the individual inhabitant' (Y.F.).

The Spatial City is a spatial structure raised on pilings that contains inhabited volumes wedged into some of its 'voids', alternating with other, unused volumes. This structure could span other unavailable sites, zones where construction is prohibited (bodies of water, swamps) or already built-up areas (an existing city). This city on stilts is a three-dimensional structure whose design is based on trihedral elements that would function by 'neighbourhood', where dwellings would be freely distributed. The superposition of levels had to allow for concentrating at just one site the industrial, residential and commercial elements of a city. Thus, Spatial City constitutes what Yona Friedman later referred to as an 'artificial topography', a sort of suspended framework that sketches out an entirely new map of the territory; a continuous, undetermined and homogeneous network, affording the city the promise of unlimited growth.

Future Systems
Jan Kaplicky (1937), Amanda Levete (1955)

Jan Kaplicky founded Future Systems in 1979, and in 1989 Amanda Levete became a partner. Together they have formed a partnership that has been described as 'setting the agenda for architecture in the 21st century.' Kaplicky trained at the College of Applied Arts and Architecture, Prague, and went on to work at Foster Associates, Piano & Rogers and Denys Lasdun and Partners. Levete trained at London's AA and gained her experience at Richard Rogers & Partners, YRM Architects and Alsop & Lyall.

From these key influences they have forged a very specific design agenda. They produce work that is not only architecturally innovative and visually striking, but also highly functional, inspired both by nature and technologies from other industries.

The practice is recognised for consistently challenging traditional concepts of space and demonstrating environmental concern and efficiency, without compromising on contemporary form. Research is a vital ingredient for the practice and a balance between experimental and real projects is kept to ensure that originality is maintained.

Among the practice's key projects are the acclaimed new NatWest Media Centre at London's Lord's Cricket Ground for MCC, a bridge linking West India Quay and Canary Wharf in London's Docklands, key urban and rural house designs, and shop designs for Comme des Garçons and Marni, in New York, Tokyo and Paris.

In 1999, Future Systems were winners of the prestigious Stirling Prize for Architecture, awarded for the NatWest Media Centre at Lord's Cricket Ground.

Selfridges, Birmingham, built, 2003

The ambition of this scheme was to design a state of the art department store that also acted as an architectural landmark for Birmingham and become a genuine catalyst for urban regeneration.

Its relationship to St Martin's church is significant, representing the religious and commercial life of the city that have evolved side by side over hundreds of years. Glimpsed from the train entering Birmingham from the south, it promises mystery and excitement in a city undergoing a 21st century renaissance.

The fluidity of shape recalls the fall of fabric or the soft lines of a body, rises from the ground and gently billows outwards before being drawn in at a kind of waistline. It then curves out again and over to form the roof, in one continuous movement. The skin is made up of thousands of aluminium discs, creating a fine, lustrous grain like the scales of a snake or the sequins of a Paco Rabanne dress. In sunlight it shimmers, reflecting minute changes in weather conditions and taking on the colours, light and shapes of people and things passing by.

The interior of Selfridges had to be a blank canvas for an array of changing interior design and shop-fits. However by designing key elements of the interior such as the dramatic roof lit atrium criss crossed by a white cat's cradle of sculpted escalators the integrity of the interior is preserved and lives up to the expectation set by the building's exterior.

Vittorio Giorgini (1926)

Florentine by birth, Vittorio Giorgini, at first under the influence of Le Corbusier and Leonardo Savioli, gradually forged his own style, which he likened to the 'architecture sculptures' by André Bloc. From the mid-1950s, Giorgini focused on researching the 'architecture of nature', i.e. the structures of natural organisms, understood as possible sources of inspiration in the realm of alternative construction techniques. As exemplified by the project for the Saldarini House (1962), it is composed entirely of a metallic trellis structure, modelled according to continuous plastic forms, then 'blocked' in concrete. In 1965, Giorgini presented his first *Manifesto of Spatiology*. He used this word to designate a type of technological innovation that could spring forth from the language of architecture by relying on structural techniques present in nature. In-depth study of the forms and functions of natural organisms allowed him to demonstrate the possibility of adopting in construction the geometric, asymmetric and curvilinear mesh structures of naturally occurring objects. In 1969, Giorgini settled in New York to teach at the Pratt Institute. He continued his research in the field of structures and architectural geometries, while undertaking parallel experimental work, often with the collaboration of his students. Giorgini's most recent works, like Hydropolis, Genesis, Walking Tall and River Crane, all extremely technological, three-dimensional structures, composed of symmetrical and asymmetrical mesh, represent the attainment of an additional level of sophistication and thereby constitute the fulfilment of his conceptual and stylistic research. In 1996, Giorgini returned to Florence, where he continues to live and work.

Organic Structures

Village and Network are part of the series of designs and models for Décors urbains futuribles (Urban and Futuristic Décors), presented in his personal exhibition in 1968 at the Palace of Diamonds in Ferrara. Here, Giorgini tackles the themes of the possible configurations for the 'city of the future', a recurring subject in the research and projects of most architects of the period. The organic composition of his cubicles for individual dwellings results in the determination of spaces with multiple and varied forms, communication between them being ensured by a series of raised passageways and surfaces. The dwellings, the same as the zones for production, spaces designed for public concourse as well as infrastructures, all become organic cells and tissue. In Network, a more geometric and regular form, Giorgini anticipates research he would later undertake in the USA, which sought to achieve the complex, geometric structure of the octahedral-tetrahedral of the octet, with which Giorgini hoped to render his theories more concrete; up to that point it was considered difficult to apply in reality and even 'utopian'.

David Greene (1937)

A founding member of Archigram with Peter Cook, David Greene chose the disappearance of architecture as one of his preferred themes. If the Living-Pod remains his major contribution to the work of Archigram, David Greene also designed many other equally radical proposals. Whereas the trend at the time was to give often spectacular expression to what was referred to as 'cybernetics' – particularly through designs for megastructures and machinery more and more influenced by modern mechanics – David Greene, conversely, had understood early on that the presence in the environment of these new technologies that were acting upon invisible fields needed to be discrete. Often presented as the group's poet,

Greene did succeed in maintaining for many years Archigram's critical perspective, which showed through in their projects, texts and images. His dream-like voice occasionally took on a somewhat disillusioned tone, and he would seek to act upon daily life by means of an ironic re-reading of it. He also was the first at Archigram to become aware of ecological and environmental issues, to which he responded by evoking visions of a utopian harmony between the artificial and the natural. Greene never ceased to insist on the disappearance of architecture in the environment, to be accomplished by means of an eruption of new technologies. A winner of several prestigious prizes, he was a universally respected professor of architecture at Westminster University in London.

Living-Pod, 1966–67

When David Greene designed the Living-Pod, man had not yet walked on the moon, but manned space flight had already successfully achieved orbit round the globe and the theme of the 'capsule' was very present in architecture. The possibility of designing an object that was at the same time vehicle, dwelling and capable of resisting harsh or unexplored environments by simulating the earth's atmosphere in an enclosed space became one of the primary challenges of experimental architecture. 'The house is a machine to bring with you, and a city is a machine where you come to plug in' (David Greene). The Living-Pod proposes this reduction of the habitat to a mere dwelling place equipped with a minimum but sufficient level of comfort. Though it was designed for earthly uses only, it nevertheless took on the aesthetics of space, its principle of adaptable hydraulic feet making it possible to set it down on unexplored ground. Moreover, the highlighting of the circulation of fluids around the envelope recalled the space suit (or helmet) of the astronaut. Greene was putting forward an argument close to the one developed by Reyner Banham with his La Maison (1965), by emphasizing the idea of the probable future abandonment of the house as a static and permanent form, to the advantage of alternative arrangements involving new technologies.

Zaha Hadid (1950)

A native of Baghdad (Iraq), Zaha Hadid began her professional life when she joined the OMA (Office for Metropolitan Architecture) of Rem Koolhaas. In 1979, she founded her own architecture firm. In 1988, she participated in the exhibition/event 'Deconstructivist Architecture' at the MoMA in New York, which also brought together under one roof Eisenman, Tschumi, Libeskind and other notables. Referring both to deconstructivism as a strategy and to Russian constructivism, Zaha Hadid invented a new imaginary universe where concept is transformed into image and the interplay of signs establishes the order of reality. Her work was already internationally recognized thanks to her first place win for The Peak in Hong Kong (1983). Hadid does not invent new forms. She reveals the world by means of new and radical graphic representations, of which her images are a part of the process leading to construction. Genuine tests of architectural role play, the project unfolds through the sketches like a storyboard. The pictorial representations are both fields of investigation and a method of exploring her architecture. Her buildings are no longer isolated objects, but result from the site, like the Fire Station in Vitra (1990–94), which appears to be an artificially constructed landscape. In a formal way, the spiral becomes a medium of spatial continuity. The Blueprint Pavilion (1995) wraps around the metallic structure like a Möbius strip; a spiral contains the volumes of the main hall in the project for the

Cardiff Opera House (1994–96). In 2001, Zaha Hadid built the Hoenheim-nord Multimodal Terminal in Strasbourg. In 2004, she won the most prestigious award in architecture, the Pritzker Prize.

The Hague Villas, Netherlands, unbuilt project, 1991

In 1991, the city of The Hague invited seven internationally renowned architects to a project of villas in one of the city's peripheral neighbourhoods. Zaha Hadid used the opportunity to attempt the definition of a new typology of the house. The first project, the Cross House, is composed of a base partially sunk into the ground and two parallelepiped volumes crossing it. The second project, the Spiral House, is developed around the idea of a perpetually ascending floor. A spiral, from the entry level to the living room, then on to the bedrooms, it rises inside a cubic volume whose limits are in turn defined by the bounds of the parcel. Spatial divisions are virtually non-existent, as the succession of spaces follows the continuity of the rising spiral. Residual spaces and voids created between the external skin and spiral generate unpredictable views and new possibilities for communication in the house.

Pascal Häusermann (1936)

A native of Bienne, Switzerland, Pascal Häusermann had already designed a cell in 1956, first in wood, which in 1958 he built without formwork in concrete sprayed directly on to a metallic armature. Häusermann used the same method from the late 1950s to develop bubbles and shells; his approach to space nowadays recalls the most futuristic topological research. In 1959, Häusermann built a house in the shape of an egg in Grilly (Ain), his first work in reinforced concrete shell without formwork. In 1966, with his wife and partner, Claude Häusermann-Costy, he used the same principle to build one of his most important works, the Balcon de Belledonne (1966), a mountain restaurant and leisure centre at Belledonne, near Chambéry, France. In 1968, he constructed numerous villas in concrete shell, including his own in Minziers. In 1966, he joined the GIAP (Groupe International d'Architecture Prospective), founded the year before by the critic Michel Ragon. In 1970, Pascal Häusermann won first prize in the Concours d'Urbanisme in Cannes with a project of cells hooked to a three-dimensional structure. An advocate of greater participation by inhabitants in the design of their environment, Häusermann also founded the association Habitat Évolutif with his friends Chanéac and Antti Lovag in 1971. He succeeded in building a Mobile Theatre (1969–71), easily dismantled and composed of two spherical cells round which micro-cells gravitated. A creative and multi-tasking figure, in the 1970s he was also the prime mover behind the restoration of the Immeuble Clarté by Le Corbusier in Geneva. Häusermann now divides his time between Geneva and Chennai, India, where he continues his research in a city that now serves as his new experimental laboratory.

Domobiles

Since 1955, Pascal Häusermann has studied the principle of Domobiles, habitats resulting from the assembly of factory-produced elements, developed using then new synthetic materials. In 1961, he explored the feasibility of cells used as dwellings and made of plastics, realizing a plastic prototype in 1962 with Eric Hoechel and Bruno Camoletti. These experiments were widely acclaimed in the press of the day, which wondered if the 'egg house was the dwelling of tomorrow'. Häusermann received many orders for Domobiles, which he was unable to fill, lacking a licence to manufacture. He and the interior architect Pascal Le Merdy nevertheless continued to develop Domobiles, which embody the principle of the adaptable habitat and mobility. The objective was to leave the freedom to adapt the dwelling to its inhabitants, who became responsible for extensions or combinations of cells. The cell served as the basic element in this modular architecture, which can evolve through the free aggregation, interconnection, stacking or juxtaposition of elements and which then fit together to form a habitable whole.

Haus-Rucker-Co (1967–92)
Laurids Ortner (1941), Manfred Ortner (1943), Günter Zamp Kelp (1941), Klaus Pinter (1940)

In 1967, the Haus-Rucker-Co was founded in Vienna by young architects and artists Laurids Ortner, Günter Zamp Kelp and Klaus Pinter. In a return to Viennese activism, their work consisted largely of performances, in which they would invest the space of the street. Haus-Rucker-Co focused on the experience of the body, developing cognitive and sensory spaces. Laurids Ortner and his team designed the Mind Expander I (1967), a veritable 'instrument for perceiving the internal world'. At the same time, Günter Zamp Kelp and Manfred Ortner imagined the Pneumacosm. Heart of Gold (1968) is an inflatable, transportable cell for several people. With the international acclaim they received, Haus-Rucker-Co, joined shortly thereafter by Manfred Ortner, opened workshops in Düsseldorf and New York (1970–71). The group was developing spatial objects, installations in urban spaces, interventions and exhibitions. For Haus-Rucker-Co, these events were intended to stimulate and liberate awareness, allowing the mind to open up to another dimension. In Vienna, in 1970, they presented their Riesenbillard (Giant Billiard Game), an enormous pneumatic environment for 100 people at the Museum of the 20th Century, later installed in the middle of a New York street. Their criticism of the notion of progress and of industrialization and its disastrous consequences for the environment became more and more virulent in the early 1970s. From 1972 onwards, the workshops were independent: Haus-Rucker, Inc. in New York (Klaus Pinter and Caroll Michels, etc.) and Haus-Rucker-Co in Düsseldorf (Laurids Ortner, Günter Zamp Kelp and Manfred Ortner). Later, in 1987, Laurids Ortner, Manfred Ortner in Vienna and Günter Zamp Kelp in Düsseldorf founded independent firms. Haus-Rucker-Co was officially dissolved in 1992 in Düsseldorf.

Pneumacosm, 1967

The group's manifesto and founding project, imagined by Günter Zamp Kelp and Manfred Ortner, Pneumacosm is an inflatable plastic unit of housing that works like an incandescent light bulb within a vertical urban structure. When a unit is 'plugged in' to the building's façade it is ready to function. One enters by means of corridors inside the building, which open to the unit. The sphere's interior divides into two areas: a large common space and several smaller spaces dedicated to various functions. These little functional units can be individually selected before their installation in the vertical structure. Thus, the sphere's internal organization gives every individual the possibility of withdrawing into the smaller cells as well as the possibility of a wider social life in the larger common space. The Pneumacosm has a transparent skin that extends the body out into the core of the city; a beating electric heart, providing the rhythm for the horizontal expansion of new urban landscapes. Here, the body becomes architecture in continual transformation.

Hans Hollein (1934)

A graduate of the Fine Arts Academy in Vienna (1956), Hollein later studied at the Illinois Institute of Technology in Chicago (1958–59) and at the University of California at Berkeley (1959–60), where he designed 'sculptural' projects, inspired by the breakaway House without End (1950) by Frederick Kiesler. His designs and projects – Monument to the Dead (1956), Project for a City as a Hub of Communications (1963), among others – demonstrated a reflection on the status of architecture, also expressed in articles and conferences, such as 'The Future of Architecture' (1965). Hollein has never shared his generation's enthusiasm for the megastructure as the means of resolving the 'problem' of the modern city in the face of 'uncontrolled' development. All forms of human production, from offshore oil rigs to nuclear explosions, found their place in 'Everything is Architecture' (1968). He has also produced collages based on changes of scale, 'Transformations', including Monument to the Victims of the Holocaust (1963), an enlarged shopping trolley. His first built works embodied association, evocation and quotation, which place him at the origins of postmodernism in architecture. His oeuvre includes several important museums.

Aeroplane Carrier City, 1964

The image of an aircraft carrier set in a landscape is a recurrent theme in Hollein's work, as seen in 'Transformations' and 'Transpositions'. 'Man today,' wrote Hollein in 1963 introducing his joint exhibition in Vienna with Walter Pichler, 'is the master of infinite space'. The aircraft carrier symbolizes the tension between human technical creation and natural space and is a metaphor for the modern city's hidden complexity and latent monumentality. The image resembles Hollein's depictions of airports and rocket launch pads.

Eilfried Huth (1930) & Günther Domenig (1934)

The careers of Huth and Domenig spread out from the city of Graz, Austria. Their earliest projects, like those of Coop Himmelb(l)au and Haus-Rucker-Co, explored the potential of inflatable structures. In 1967, for the Trigon show, they perfected a pneumatic exhibition hall. In 1969, with the Ragnitz project, they developed one of the most significant designs for megastructures in the history of contemporary architecture. The experimental approach followed by Huth and Domenig achieved a decisive mutation, characteristic of the radical architecture of the period: architecture became a cognitive field, eschewing its status as frozen object to be transfigured into environment. Following their Artiflex project (1967–72), they built the Olympics Pavilion (Swimming Hall) in Munich (1970–72), an organic agglomeration of cells, as well as the Multipurpose Hall in Graz-Eggenberg (1974–77) with its biomorphic shapes. Joint winners of numerous prizes, Huth and Domenig also built the Pädagogische Akademie der Diozese Graz-Seckau (Graz-Seckau Diocesan Educational Academy), Graz-Eggenberg, in 1964–69, a building that explores avenues of a New Brutalism. After their separation in 1973, each pursued a rich career as architect and professor. Günther Domenig counted among his major projects the transformation of his own home, beginning in 1986. The Steinhaus (Stone House) work in progress was a laboratory and/or living organism in perpetual evolution. An archetypal architecture, the Steinhaus upsets all of one's ordinary markers for daily living in the house, with, for example, interlocking metal 'boulders' tossed on top of each other. Throughout the 1980s and 1990s, their works were the subject of numerous exhibitions.

Ragnitz, Austria, unbuilt project, 1965

In 1965, Huth and Domenig received the commission for a project to develop the Ragnitz valley, which in the end was refused. However, their project did win the Grand Prix d'Urbanisme et d'Architecture in 1969 in Cannes, and from an exceptional jury comprised of, among others, Louis Kahn, Jean Prouvé, Robert Le Ricolais, J.B. Bakema, S.Z. Makowsky and Bruno Zevi. Reyner Banham wrote in his book *Megastructure, Urban Futures of the Recent Past* (1976) that Ragnitz was, for him, the richest and most accomplished of all the megastructures. In its complexity, scope and radical nature, Ragnitz holds a special place in the wake of the 'Villes spatiales' (Spatial Cities) of Yona Friedman, beginning in 1958, and later works such as the Pompidou Centre in Paris by Piano and Rogers, in the 1970s, which owe so much to it. The city of the megastructure is defined by its capacity of infinite expansion, its modularity, its freedom in terms of planning, thanks to its open infrastructure. The urban space becomes a network of clusters or free settlements of dwelling-cells. Architecture means industrially prefabricated infrastructure, into which spatial cells composed of synthetic materials for circulation and dwelling can be incorporated.

Arata Isozaki (1931)

Arata Isozaki was born in Oita Prefecture. After graduating from the University of Tokyo in 1954, he joined Kenzo Tange's firm and worked on the design side of Tange's projects. In the first half of the 1960s, this included the megastructure-like A Plan for Tokyo (1960) and other projects closely aligned with the Metabolism movement. As a result, Isozaki is often associated with the megastructure aspects of Metabolism and mistakenly categorized as a Metabolist. In Kukan-e (Towards Space), he explains that he did not become a member of the Metabolists 'simply because I started too late'.1 Nevertheless, the urban planning approach he took for the Joint Core System he exhibited at the Seibu Department Store in 1962 differed not at all from the approach of the Metabolists. There is no doubting the similarity of his methodology, but Isozaki set himself apart from other Metabolist architects by adding images of ruins and images of uncompleted projects.

In 1963 he established Arata Isozaki & Associates, and a succession of projects for Isozaki followed, including the Oita Prefectural Library (1966) and the Oita Branch of Fukuoka Mutual Bank (1967). Whether local projects in his native Oita City or international projects around the world, Isozaki's work was highly rated. He has done some particularly notable designs for art museums, including the Gunma Museum of Fine Arts (1974), the Kitakyushu City Museum of Arts (1974) and the LA Museum of Contemporary Art (1986). Many other projects have been completed in Japan, and, at the time of writing, he is working on several similar projects internationally. Recently he has turned his attention to China, holding exhibitions and working on art museum design projects, and he has gained an international reputation as an architect with a Japanese artistic orientation.

Isozaki has a particularly strong grasp of art, music and the history of architecture, and is known for his very conceptual approach, his architecture incorporating clever allusions to such non-architectural contexts. This may be seen, for example, in his 'MA: Space-Time in Japan' exhibition (1978). The composition of the exhibition was an attempt to be aware of and rationalize Japanese spaces, and it was highly rated from the perspective of cultural theory. Isozaki is also a prolific writer and it

is to him that we owe the solid record of post-war discourse on architecture
in Japan.

Clusters in the Air Project, proposal, 1960–62

In the second half of the 1960s, Isozaki wrote about the Invisible City, describing
a fictitious city stretching into mid-air and consisting of a grouping of propagable
buildings similar to the megastructures of Metabolism. Infrastructure towers fulfilled
the function of lifelines and roads, and the units that comprise the buildings were
inserted into the spaces between the towers. Clusters in the Air was a proposal for
the redevelopment of Shinjuku. This was just one of the many ideas that architects
produced for Shinjuku in the 1960s, but Isozaki's was special in providing the
infrastructure through vertical towers (called the joint core) and propagating
the structure by adding architectural units as and when required. This is what
Archigram would call a plug-in system, and has a lot in common with the thinking
behind Le Corbusier's unités d'habitation. A tower standing alone is architecture,
but if there is a whole thicket of such towers making a joint structure, the result is
a city. The vertical infrastructure approach was a break from conventional cities,
and Isozaki combined this proposal with new virtual cities spreading out from
the vertical infrastructure. The idea incorporates a utopian vision of a new frontier
or new land being created in the air by superimposing the new structure on to
an existing city. This concept is currently bearing fruit in Doha, Qatar, where
construction is in progress for the Qatar National Library and the Qatar National
Bank.

Jakob & MacFarlane
Dominique Jakob (1966) & Brendan MacFarlane (1961)

The architecture of Jakob & MacFarlane, though it can be qualified as contextual,
is not concerned with a sociological or historical context, but refers to an attempt
to redefine the programme. Hence, in the restaurant Georges (2000), in the
Pompidou Centre in Paris, behind its formal 'bubble' appearance, which houses
the restaurant's functions, it is the guiding principle of Piano and Rogers that
reappears, referring the public back to a critical awareness of the architectural
environment. This critical dimension characterizes the realizations of Jakob &
MacFarlane. The raised Maison T (La Garenne-Colombes, 1998) freely and openly
recomposes space. Their project for the World Trade Center is filled with the
flexibility of the vegetal, in a denunciation of representational architecture of
permanence. Their built work always refuses the architectonic. The roof of the
Centre de Communication de Renault (2002) is a multiplication of mobile plates,
creating the effect of motion, as a sort of parasitism of the gigantic open plan
they cover. Jakob & MacFarlane projects are open spaces for liberty, in which the
architects redefine the scope of their practice and implement methods for new
types of intervention.

Docks de Paris, City of Mode and Design, 2005–2007

The Docks of Paris is a long thin concrete building built at the turn of the last
century. It was a depot for goods brought up the Seine by barge later transferred
to dray or train. Jakob & MacFarlane's will retain the existing structure and uses it
to form and influence the new design. The concept is called 'Plug-Over'. A new
external skin to protect the existing structure and form a new layer for most of the
public circulation systems is proposed, that will also create a new top floor. A tree-

generating method will create a new system, 'growing' the new onto the old just as new branches grow on a tree. The exterior skin is a glass and steel structure with wood decking and a prairie faceted roofscape.

The new pattern forms a continuous loop from the lowest level by the river to the roof deck and back down, allowing it to become part of the cityscape. The building complex is a rich mix centred on the theme of design and fashion, including exhibition spaces, a French fashion institute, music studios, bookshops, cafes and a restaurant.

Jones, Partners: Architecture
Wes Jones (1958)

Wes Jones studied at the University of California, Berkeley (1980) and Harvard Graduate School of Design (1983) and in 1985 received the American Academy in Rome's prize. In San Francisco in 1993 he founded Jones Partners Architecture, later installed in Los Angeles. His prize-winning project for the memorial for the astronauts killed in the Challenger space shuttle disaster (Astronauts Memorial, Kennedy Space Center, Florida, 1988) was awarded the annual prize from the review *Progressive Architecture*. This memorial bears witness to the 'architecture-machine' that has interested Wes Jones since the 1980s and which he continues to explore. However, his work on projects cannot be separated from his significant work in criticism and theory. The multiplication of motorized mobile organizations, use of structures or machinery generally associated with construction sites, borrowing vehicular models or rejection of foundation works in favour of a leverage system are a few of the architectonic elements characterizing the numerous projects realized by Wes Jones and which contribute to the definition of an aesthetic register associating mechanics and mobility. By openly displaying mechanical components, his projects suggest a sort of updating of one of the major dimensions of architectural modernity derived from historical avant-gardes: architecture as machine. But these mechanical components, which introduce a reflection on the presence of the technological and architectural object in time, also signal the paradoxes of this updating, thereby referring back to the essential dimension of criticism.

Primitive Hut Models, proposal 1998

The variations on the classical theme of man's first shelters, symbol of the Vitruvian tradition and myth of the 'natural' origins of architecture, have obvious value as paradigmatic declaration. These cabins suggest the logic of primitivism coming from technological modernity and equipment allowing for the deployment of the mechanical and architectonic elements of Wes Jones's vocabulary: leveraging systems, simply placed on the ground, as opposed to the naturalist tradition of putting down roots; access ramps referring to vehicular forms, to situations of transit, very remote from images of sedentary dwellings; protection systems evoking exaggerated mechanical forces. This declaration of intent is therefore a comment on the very notion of shelter and its variations in an innovative tradition of modern architecture (from the reduced cells of the housing with the 'minimum vital' requirements from the 1920s, all the way to the capsules of the 1960s). This replay of the founding myth also refers to a reflection on the habitat and the status of body/inhabitant.

Kiyonori Kikutake (1928)

Kiyonori Kikutake was born in 1928 in Fukuoka Prefecture. He established his own firm of architects in 1953, and in 1960 was one of the founding members of the Metabolism movement. In the 1950s, Japan shook off the chaos of the immediate post-war period and started on a path of economic growth. When it was decided to hold the 1960 World Design Conference in Japan, Kikutake and the other members of the hosting committee set about preparing a manifesto for the world's architects, which resulted in the publication METABOLISM/1960. Kikutake's Marine City Project (1958) and Tower-shaped Community (1958) became the best-known images of the Metabolists' proposals for future cities. Kikutake's works include the Administrative Building of Izumo Shrine (1963), Hotel Toko-en (1964), Pacific Hotel Chigasaki (1967) and Osaka Expo Tower (1970). One of the clearest manifestations of this sort of union between modernity and Japanese culture was Kikutake's own house, Sky House (1958). It had the spaces arranged in two planes, the design of the central living room being rooted in the traditions of the Japanese room (Nihon-ma). The house had the flexibility to add or remove rooms to handle changes in family composition. In fact, the traditional architecture of the Japanese room and the principles of space usage that it embodies are part of the background to the magnificent marine cities that Kikutake designed.

In *Ningen no Toshi* (*Human City*; 1970), Kikutake argues that a Western room is a form in which spaces are constrained by things, whereas in Japanese rooms the constraints on spaces are imposed by information. The Asakawa Apartment House (1964) is an example of an extension of this principle of space to collective housing. Following that were the redevelopment of areas alongside the Den'en Toshi railway line that runs through Tokyo suburbs, and different experiments for Pair City, published together in *Toshi Jukyo no Sai-kochiku* (*Rebuilding Urban Housing*). These designs for collective housing are essentially a manifestation of the process of making a reality of the high-density urban housing images drawn by the Metabolists. Recent works by Kikutake include Edo-Tokyo Museum (1993), Hotel COSIMA (now known as Hotel Sofitel Tokyo; 1994) and Kyushu National Museum (2004).

Marine City Project, proposal, 1958–63

Debate on urban design in 1950s Japan was still at a very early stage when Kikutake's images of future cities appeared on the scene. First came Tower-shaped Community, published in 1959 in *Kokusai Kenchiku* magazine, a megastructure city model that was developed further to become the Marine City Series. Each of the models had a man-made foundation, a concept permitting space units to be added or removed according to circumstances and an image of a city that is endlessly regenerating and growing, displaying metabolism like that of living things. The Marine City model of 1963 followed on from Marine City 'Unabara'. Kikutake continued to make related proposals, including Marine City 1968, Hawaii Floating City (1971), Aquapolis (1975), Floating Hotel Plan (1977), and Inland Sea Linear City (1993). Each of these images of future cities envisaged lifestyles based on Japanese traditions, culture and customs, while attempting to answer questions raised by high-density cities of the near future – how people will live their daily lives and relate to each other and how they will formalize relationships between private and public and between ideas and forms.

KOL/MAC Studio
Sulan Kolatan (1958) & William Mac Donald (1956)

The KOL/MAC Studio architectural practice, founded in New York in 1988, committed itself to taking into account all the complexity of contemporary life, and to achieve this seized upon information technologies. Both architects teach at Columbia University, where they develop an architectural practice in which they continually seek to experiment with the formal and conceptual limits of the discipline. They endeavour to go beyond old mechanistic models by developing methodologies inspired by information theory: the 'co-citation maps' and the 'chimerical hybrids' are project tools they have developed for providing architecture with the possibility of opening up new and unexplored or even unthinkable territories. KOL/MAC observed that, '[A]rchitecture is competing in both the cultural and commercial fields, with the superior powers of thematic environments, branded products, advertising, the Web and its industries of music and movies.' They therefore intend to implement a different scenario, in which architecture 'adapts to these new paradigms by co-operating with all of them on whatever scale is possible in order to form precise and selective "chimerical" tactical systems with the categories involved'. Architecture in the age of globalization can act as an incentive for new mixes and hybridizations at every level of society. In 2000, they designed the Resi-Rise Skyscraper in New York. This luxurious and improbable construction of flexible coffers or cabins reinterprets the 'capsule-architecture' of the Japanese Metabolists of the 1960s. Computer graphic tools have finally enabled the emergence of an integral 'organicism' in which materials and forms meld into one.

Rem Koolhaas (1944)

Born in Rotterdam, Netherlands, Rem Koolhaas studied at the Architectural Association School in London from 1968 to 1972. He developed two theoretical projects during this period: in 1970, The Berlin Wall as Architecture, and in 1972, with Elia and Zoé Zenghelis and Madelon Vriesendorp, Exodus or the Voluntary Prisoners of Architecture, a demonstration, by the absurd, of the culpability of architectural ideology. From 1973 to 1976, living mainly in New York, he began to write the book in which he analysed the impact of metropolitan culture on architecture: *Delirious New York: A Retroactive Manifesto for Manhattan*. The work was first published in 1978 in New York, London and Paris. Taking as his point of departure the most elaborate existing built form, the metropolis, Koolhaas succeeds in isolating architecture's quintessence and condensing it into a single entity, thereby demonstrating that Manhattan engendered its very own urbanism: the 'culture of congestion'. In 1975, and back in Europe, Koolhaas founded the OMA (Office for Metropolitan Architecture) with Elia and Zoé Zenghelis and Madelon Vriesendorp in London. The OMA chose as its programme the definition of new modes of relationships, theoretical as much as practical, between architecture and the contemporary cultural situation. In 1978, they opened an office in Rotterdam. Most of their buildings can be considered as research projects. The firm is first and foremost a laboratory constantly focused on finding solutions for the new problems facing a society characterized by overpopulation and instability. In parallel, the house is a part of the OMA's reflection on the contemporary city: the Villa dell'Ava (1992) in St. Cloud, the house in Bordeaux, the Dutch House and Patiovilla all develop new uses and lifestyles. In 2000, Rem Koolhaas won the most prestigious international architectural award, the Pritzker Prize.

Exodus or the Voluntary Prisoners of Architecture, 1972

Once, a city was divided in two parts.

One part became the Good Half, the other part the Bad Half.

The inhabitants of the Bad Half began to flock to the good part of the divided city, rapidly swelling into an urban exodus.

If this situation had been allowed to continue for ever, the population of the Good Half would have doubled, while the Bad Half would have turned into a ghost town.

After all attempts to interrupt this undesirable migration had failed, the authorities of the bad part made desperate and savage use of architecture: they built a wall around the good part of the city, making it completely inaccessible to their subjects.

The Wall was a masterpiece.

Originally no more than some pathetic strings of barbed wire abruptly dropped on the imaginary line of the border, its psychological and symbolic effects were infinitely more powerful than its physical appearance. The Good Half, now glimpsed only over the forbidding obstacle from an agonising distance, became even more irresistible. Those trapped, left behind in the gloomy Bad Half, became obsessed with vain plans for escape. Hopelessness reigned supreme on the wrong side of the Wall.

As so often before in this history of mankind, architecture was the guilty instrument of despair.

The City of the Captive Globe, 1972

Archipelago of blocks, *The City of the Captive Globe* illustrates Manhattan's culture of congestion. In the centre, in a cube, the global city rises up to the rhythm of its maturing ideas, each of which has city blocks for a base. Though these remain unfinished, they adopt an informal structure, with indefinite contours. 'Each Science or Mania has its own plot [...] From these solid blocks of granite, each philosophy has the right to expand indefinitely toward heaven [...] The collapse of one of the towers can mean two things: failure, giving up, or a visual Eureka, a speculative ejaculation.' Sprinkled with allusions to the grid of the Plan Voisin (Neighbourhood Plan) by Le Corbusier, as well as suprematist theories of the architectones by Malevitch, *The City of the Captive Globe* is a purely mental construction, dominated by the infinite repetition of the grid, which absorbs all urbanism, thereby guaranteeing the system's immutability.

Flagrante Delicto, 1975

Flagrante Delicto, designed in 1975 by Madelon Vriesendorp, and of which another version executed in 1978 (coll. Frankfurt Museum of Architecture) would later appear on the cover of the retroactive manifesto *Delirious New York*, borrows its dreamlike imaginary world from its surrealist heritage, as well as from Pop Art. Here, fantastic stories cohabit with fragments of reality, inhabited by a mutant and symbiotic body. The city reveals its machine-like subconscious and the skyscrapers become a forest of 'desiring machines'. The iconography of *Flagrante Delicto* also subscribes to Freudian dream mechanisms that function through displacement and condensation. In this nocturnal scene, two skyscrapers are surprised together in bed. Outside, 'voyeuristic' skyscrapers conjure up the 'paranoid –critical conquest' by Salvador Dalí. The work is an anamnesis of architecture, proceeding through clusters of local and disjointed memories, an echo of the 'blocks' that, jammed together, constitute the urban archipelago. For Koolhaas, the architect implies s/he is manipulated by the unconscious forces of a culture. 'Manhattanism' is portrayed as a 'technology of fantasy', whose transformations obey the rules of the life of the psyche. Architecture, as depicted through the two anthropomorphic skyscrapers, is freed of its subconscious mind, which is lying on the floor, just this side of the bed, in the form of a grid. Liberated from architecture, the grid is alone, as if it had finally rid itself of its architectural super-ego.

Kisho Kurokawa (1934)

Born in Aichi Prefecture, Kisho Kurokawa was a key member of the Metabolism Group, and remains one of the best-known architects in Japan today. In 1960, when Kurokawa worked on the preparations for the World Design Conference, he had already studied under Kenzo Tange, having just completed his Masters in Architecture in 1959 and become, at 26, the youngest member of the Metabolism Group. On the strength of his Agricultural City proposal (1960), the young Kurokawa was invited, along with Kiyonori Kikutake, to exhibit in MoMA's 'Visionary Architecture' exhibition in New York (1960). Agricultural City featured mushroom-shaped buildings comprising living areas and areas for common facilities. Kurokawa took the lead in formalizing the theoretical methodology of Metabolism, and continued to push forward its ideas, evolving practical solutions by using capsules to group individuals together. Other designs include Isogo Housing Complex Plan (1962). His approach can still be seen today, in Nakagin Capsule Tower in Shinbashi (1972) and the National Ethnological Museum (1977). In 1980, Kurokawa began to put particular emphasis on the idea of symbiosis and the sublation of Japanese methods to overcome differences between Japan and the West or between tradition and modernity through architecture's diachronicity (architecture as a continuously changing process) and its synchronicity (dismantling of Western modernity; Japan/East Asia symbiosis on equal terms), which resulted in Kurokawa's establishing his own methodology.

Helix City Plan for Tokyo, proposal, 1961

This plan was drawn up for publication in the second Metabolism manifesto (which was never actually published). It took its inspiration from the double-helix structure of DNA in chromosomes, metamorphosing into a life-related metaphor utilized by the Metabolists. The plan was for high-rise architecture, with man-made land created by bridging the double spiral strands to become dynamic mid-air gardens. The whole city had redevelopment areas and preservation areas bounded by ring roads that formed networks for traffic and infrastructure. The combination of expansion on horizontal planes and vertical propagation gives the architecture a firm sense of being an imposing city of the future. Floating City, Kasumigaura (1961), was conceived as an application of the Helix City Plan, introducing the variation of a man-made foundation floating on the lake. The structure pushed outwards, with doors opening in three different directions from a single axis, linking together and growing in a flexible manner.

Project for Box-type Mass-produced Apartments, proposal, 1962

This plan conceived of collective housing as box-shaped core units that could be repeated continually and that could be manufactured by mass production. The whole structure was composed of living units, with the living space located in the centre, and space for storage and for equipment and facilities located around the edge. These units were propagated laterally and vertically, producing an overlapping awareness of two sorts of space – the physical units and the integrated space. Expo 70 Theme Pavilion in Osaka (1970) was an extension of this idea, the space under its gigantic roof being divided into four themes. The exhibition area and small areas for other functions were suspended from space frames, so as to be subordinate to the main space.

Daniel Libeskind (1946)

Internationally recognized as the architect of the new World Trade Center in New York, as well as for the construction of the Jewish Museum in Berlin (1989–99), the Felix Nussbaum Museum in Osnabrück, Germany (1995–2001), the design for the San Francisco Jewish Museum (1998–2005) and for the extension of the Victoria & Albert Museum in London (1996–2004), Daniel Libeskind, born in Lodz, Poland, and an American citizen since 1965, arrived in New York in 1960. It was here that he became interested in mathematics, painting and eventually architecture, obtaining his diploma in that field in 1970 at the Cooper Union in New York with John Hejduk. Libeskind emphasizes the project design over its actual construction, his singular research first being the subject of design exhibitions and theoretical productions across the globe. In 1988, he participated in the seminal exhibition at the MoMA in New York, 'Deconstructivist Architecture', beside architects such as Peter Eisenman, Zaha Hadid and Coop Himmelb(l)au. Coming from a family wiped out in the concentration camps, Libeskind invests memory with an essential role in his projects, injecting a deeply emotional and symbolic charge into them. From his perspective, history is not about a past condemned to be forgotten, but rather part of an evolving and unpredictable process activating the present between the future and the past. Libeskind incorporates into his projects a fundamental questioning of the world's destiny. Based in Berlin, Libeskind's firm is developing numerous urban projects for this city and has recently completed the design for the Maurice Wohl Convention Centre in Tel Aviv, as well as the extension of the Denver Museum in Colorado and the Royal Ontario Museum in Toronto.

City Edge, Urban Competition, Berlin, unbuilt project, 1987

Designed in 1987 the City Edge project aimed to rehabilitate part of the Tiergarten neighbourhood in then West Berlin, which had suffered severe destruction during the war and required a new urban organization. The two models were presented as a simultaneously historic, literary and philosophical reflection on Berlin. The collages covering them transformed them into a sort of palimpsest containing half-hidden allusions to Joyce, Benjamin or even the Talmud. Traces of Albert Speer's Berlin of the Nazi period appear as stigmata. One of his models materializes Berlin with its 75 million cubic metres of debris, accumulated during the war, and which probably served as 'foundations' for present-day Berlin, thus raised by nearly 28 metres owing to its reconstruction on its own ruins. The two versions of this project also included an oblique block of flats overlooking the Berlin wall, thereby negating its very existence.

C.J. Lim + Studio 8 Architects
C.J. Lim (1964)

Born in Ipoh, Malaysia, C.J. Lim arrived in England in 1981. Having graduated from the Architectural Association and the Royal Institute of British Architects (RIBA), he spent a year as assistant to Zaha Hadid, Eva Jiricna, Peter Cook and Christine Hawley and in 1994 founded Studio 8 Architects in London. His intense and varied practice includes teaching and work as a theoretician as well as developing a forward-looking architecture. He has taught in numerous architectural schools since 1989. He has directed the Bartlett Architecture Research Lab at London's Bartlett School since 1993. Having won numerous prizes, in 1997 he became the first recipient of the RIBA Award for Academic Contribution in Architectural Education. His work has been shown in exhibitions in France, the USA, Italy (2000 Venice Biennale) and Canada. One of the most important exhibitions – '441/10 ... we'll reconfigure the space when you're ready' – was followed by the book of the same title, published in 1996. C.J. Lim recently wrote *Realms of Impossibility* (2002) in three volumes, in which the same story is told three times in the different contexts of air, land and water, like the Guest House project.

Guest House, The Landscape + Environmental Register, Japan, unbuilt project, 1995

The Guest House can exist in any context, to which it responds by changing shape: aquatic, terrestrial or subterranean. The house is formally unstable, flexible. Sensory envelope, intelligent membrane and hypersurface that can be programmed around the choices of its occupants and the outside environment, it places the inhabitant in an interactive world. The architecture becomes reactive and receptive to real-time weather conditions. C.J. Lim turns the environment into an instrument for inventing fictional space and unusual events. The house exists in a constant state of metamorphosis from sunrise to sunset. Its spaces are totally interchangeable according to the situation: a door becomes a floor, a bed becomes a wall. The house is transformed into a dismembered cinematic body, breaking down space into linear series that conjure up images of the chronophotographs of Etienne-Jules Marey. C.J. Lim's Guest House owes a great deal to the floating and flying cities envisaged by Buckminster Fuller, Archigram and the Metabolists.

Antti Lovag (1920)

Born in Hungary, Antti Lovag settled in France in 1947, after living in Turkey, Finland and Sweden and serving as a pilot in World War II. Beginning in 1963, he worked alongside Jacques Couëlle, one of the first French architects to develop organic architecture. In 1970, he began working with Chanéac and Häusermann on projects for collective adaptable housing; together, they developed the interconnecting cells that were adaptable according to the desires of their inhabitants. In 1969, to convince a client, he elaborated a 1:1 scale model of a house in Tourrettes-sur-Loup (Nice), in which he lives to this day. Concrete shells were sprayed on a particular type of reinforcement or concrete reinforced with fibres to develop cylindrical and spherical spaces, using techniques involving notably reinforcements and soldered trellises in a process called 'tricot tendu' ('stretched knit'), i.e. composed of arcs over which a membrane was stretched. The craft of fabricating these shells relied on the research carried out by engineers in the 1950s–1960s on applications for reinforced concrete shells in architecture. More interested in humans than in architecture for its own sake, Antti Lovag calls himself not an architect but a 'habitologue'. 'Architecture does not interest me.

It is man, the human species that interests me; creating an envelope around man's needs. I work as tailor, I make bespoke envelopes, envelopes whose shapes can be changed at will.' Antti Lovag also involved users in the design of his spaces, proclaiming the principle of do-it-yourself construction.

Espace Cardin (Pierre Cardin's Bubble Palace), Théoule-sur-Mer, built, 1993

Coiled on the heights overlooking Théoule-sur-Mer, near Cannes, Pierre Cardin's Bubble Palace in l'Esquillon (1993) is an arrangement of interconnecting spheres, staggered over several levels. There is not a right angle visible in the entire place, only hemispheres poking out to envelop without closing space. 'Sky domes', or oculi, cut out at mid-level or directly overhead, integrate the architecture in a softer, more intimate way into the surrounding landscape. The furnishings, an essential element in bubble houses, are entirely designed by Antti Lovag, including the famous banquette in the shape of an arc circling around its central pivot. In this edifice, the exterior translates the interior. The fluidity of the spaces opens up new perceptions of the body and its environment. Antti Lovag's bubble houses seek the right adaptation to nature, like a living being.

Gordon Matta-Clark (1943–1978)

A major figure in the history of art of the last 40 years, Gordon Matta-Clark began his career in the artistic context of the early 1970s. His conceptual approach benefited from the critical analysis he applied stemming from his training as architect. Working on constructed space in the 1970s, he transformed architectural elements into sculptural objects. With his giant blows to the roof, flooring and walls of a building, testing the resistance of its materials in an almost expressionist manner, Gordon Matta-Clark not only anticipated the future destruction of the architectural framework and envelope but also experimented with a principle of deconstruction. His work manifests his interest in analysing man's relationship to his urban environment. Beginning in 1971, he built installations *in situ* and started intervening in constructed space (Food); Thereafter, his work would consist of cutting up buildings slated for demolition. Splitting (1974), Conical Intersect (1975), Office Baroque (1977) were all works based on bringing ignored and unknown strata to light, revealing the specific history of a place and the internal structure of its building. Gordon Matta-Clark offered new experiences of the urban space by way of an opened and destabilizing experience of buildings. He was described as 'the only true Deconstructivist architect' (James Wines, 'The Slippery Floor', in A. Papadakis (ed.), *Deconstruction*, Academy Editions, London, 1989).

Office Baroque, Antwerp, 1977

Office Baroque results from a series of over 20 photographs taken during an intervention by the artist in Antwerp in 1977. Comprising several Cibachrome prints, in the form of hand-cut contact sheets, the series follows a work in progress *in situ* taken from several angles. It is the photographic memory of action shot as it occurred, in the same way as film or video would be used by other artists executing analogous ephemeral operations. This photographic work was realized on a five-storey administrative building slated for demolition, located in one of the city's most popular tourist neighbourhoods. The cuts crossing the building from top to bottom follow a formal progression, starting with the circle and finishing in curving sections in the shape of a small boat. By upsetting the instantaneous comprehension of a space and its overall impact 'in one glance', Matta-Clark disorients the regard, compelling it to follow a perilous physical path. He cuts into the material to allow an 'additional' view, that of social and historical realities, on strata of its history hitherto invisible. It is by creating these cutaway voids, by the will to link the ground and the ceiling, that a deeply sensory experiment allows visitors to grasp the architectural thinking and internal complexity of the building. The construction procedure marches in reverse, undertaken with all the rigour of an engineer, bringing to light the neurological forces of the edifice.

Morphosis
Thom Mayne (1944) & Michael Rotondi (1949)
In 1971, Thom Mayne and Michael Rotondi (who left the firm in 1992) created Morphosis. One of the first issues of the Japanese review *GA Houses* brought them international recognition in 1985. In the early days, in the absence of competitions, Morphosis, like other US firms, concentrated on realizing programmes for additions to individual houses, in their case in Venice Beach and Santa Monica. The 6th House, which took several years to complete, earned them invaluable media attention. The house bears witness to the interest Morphosis have in the performance of the metallurgy industry: indeed, it incorporates metallic elements right down to the steel furniture and washbasins in perforated sheet metal. Destabilization, fractured or lacerated spaces, oblique walls and suspended architectonic elements represent just some of many manipulations of form that situate Morphosis in the movement of what was and still is too swiftly referred to as architectural deconstruction. Co-founder with Rotondi, in Los Angeles, in 1972 of the school of architecture SCI-Arc, known for its experimental approach, Thom Mayne has taught at UCLA since 1993. He continues with Morphosis to undertake projects in the USA (Diamond Ranch High School, Pomona; the New Federal Building, San Francisco), Mexico, Japan, Korea and in Europe (the Hypobank, in Austria, housing in Madrid).

Malibu Beach House, unbuilt project, 1987–88
Situated on a narrow parcel of land facing the Pacific Ocean, the house is divided lengthwise in two parts. The azure surface of the tides' ceaseless ebb and flow appears in the model. For Morphosis, models function as both conceptual and aesthetic experiments. A decomposition of grids, the house is built on pilings and opens to its environment. A reference to the 1930s Casa del Fascio by Terragni and the language of the Modernist architects, the Malibu Beach House is also one of the most representative examples of deconstruction.

Eric Owen Moss (1943)
A native of Los Angeles, Eric Owen Moss has built a number of his projects in Culver City, California, where he lives and works. Having graduated from the University of California, Berkeley, in 1968 and Harvard University in 1972, he founded his own firm, Eric Owen Moss Architects, in 1973 and is now Professor at the Southern California Institute of Architecture (SCI-Arc). He has been awarded numerous prizes. In his early projects, houses essentially, he analysed the interpenetration of geometric entities – circle, cube and cone – and the consequences of this for the construction of space, so often subject to unexpected distortions. From Petal House (Los Angeles, 1982–84) to Mills House (Hollywood, 1998) by way of Metafor (1991–95), the Lawson/Westen House (1988) and the P&D Guest House (Tarzana, California, 1991), Moss implements complex and flexible space and

abolishes the separation between exterior and interior. In Culver City, west of Los Angeles, Moss undertook vast structural rehabilitation projects, mainly of former warehouses. Thus he realized the Paramount Laundry Building, Lindblade Tower, Gary Group Complex, office projects, cultural institutions, theatres, galleries, restaurants, collective and single-family housing, all between 1987 and 1990. More recently, he built Beehive (2002).

MVRDV

The practice MVRDV was formed in 1991 in Rotterdam by Winy Maas, Jacob van Rijs and Nathalie de Vries. MVRDV produces, designs and studies architecture, urbanism and landscape design. Early projects such as the Light Urbanism study for the Municipality of Rotterdam, the headquarters for the Public Broadcasting Company VPRO and housing for elderly WoZoCos in Amsterdam brought their work to international attention.

The office continues to pursue its fascination with and methodical research into density. It uses a method of shaping space through complex amounts of data that accompany contemporary building and design processes. MVRDV have published numerous books, including FARMAX (1998).

Realized projects include the Dutch Pavilion for the World Expo in 2000 in Hanover; an innovative business 'Flight Forum' in Eindhoven, the Silodam Housing Complex in Amsterdam, the Matsudai Cultural Centre in Japan, two Houses at Borneo Sporenbrug in Amsterdam, offices in Unterforung Munich, the Lloyd Hotel in Amsterdam, as well as an urban plan and housing in Ypenburg and the futuristic installation Metacity/Datatown that is travelling around the world.

Pig City, 2001

In 2000, pork was the most consumed form of meat at 80 billion kg per year. Recent animal diseases such as swine fever and Foot and Mouth Disease are raising serious questions about pork production and consumption.

Two opposing reactions can be imagined. Either we change our consumption pattern and become instant vegetarians or we change the production methods and demand biological farming.

Let us assume that we remain pork eaters. Do we then have enough space for biological pig farming?

With a production of 16.5 million tons of pork, The Netherlands is the chief pork exporter within the European Union. In the case of organic farming, pigs would be fed with 100% grain, leading to a required 130% more field surface due to the reduced grain production. This would mean that 75% of the Netherlands would be dedicated to pigs.

Pig City studies the combination of organic farming with a further concentration of the meat production area, avoiding unnecessary transportation and distribution, and thereby reducing the spread of diseases.

NOX
Lars Spuybroek (1959)

Rotterdam-based NOX have explored the relationship between architecture and the media. They have developed a flexible kind of architecture, drawing from both the universe of biological organisms and that of digital technologies. Faced with the 'liquefaction' of the world, the transformation of material by media, forms and space by information, for NOX everything is involved in a process of transformation. The liquid in architecture signifies not only generating the geometry of the fluid and the turbulent, but also dissolving the functional and the programmatic. NOX leaves behind the mechanistic apprehension of the body for a more plastic, liquid and haptic approach in which action and vision are synthesized. Drawing on philosophy (Merleau-Ponty), poetry (Poe, Blake, Rimbaud) and neurology (Oliver Sacks, Francisco Varela), NOX apprehend movement as 'indissociable from bodily structure'. They designed Pavilion H2O eXPO, V2-lab and wetGRID, and their current work includes an interactive project for the city of Doetinchem (D-Tower), 'a house where sounds have a life' (Son-O-House), an office building in Warwickshire, England (SoftOffice), a cultural complex and the MaisonFOLIE (2001–03) realized in Lille, as well as
a Pavilion for Alice in Wonderland (Roberto Masiero/Carlo Collodi Foundation, 2001–04). Calling for a 'non-standard constructivism', NOX continue to pursue a close association between design and manufacturing technology.

Soft Office, Warwickshire, UK, unbuilt project, 2000

Designed in the beginning for a television production company, the project consisted of associating office spaces with play areas for children. NOX borrowed new techniques from Frei Otto to imagine these spaces, as the models clearly show: in one case, rubber tubes are coated in lacquer, creating a porous Swiss cheese-like surface, which determines the distribution of the spaces; in the other, the soaked wool yarn draws a sort of liquid substance that blends into the landscape. Once digitized, the models will become the referents for the project, which is presented as an incursion into the field of the metamorphosis of architectural forms.

Objectile (1995)
Bernard Cache (1952) & Patrick Beaucé (1960)

Paris-based Objectile functions as a sort of laboratory, which intervenes in the core of software programmes for computer-assisted design and fabrication. The team's singularity, in the architectural landscape, resides in their simultaneous engagement on two fronts, i.e. the theoretical and the practical. Moreover, it is no accident that Objectile defines its work as the 'pursuit of philosophy by other means'. Objectile attracted attention during the first ArchiLab show in 1999 with a 1:1 scale construction of the Semper Pavilion, the first example of 'associative' architecture, which was followed by the Pavilion de l'Orme (2001). Its presence in the FRAC Centre collection stands out because of a series of wood panels carved by a digitally operated milling machine. There is no architectural model, nor any elevation of a programme to build. For Objectile, no architecture is possible without fundamental questioning about ornament and form. Hence, Cache's research endeavours to return to living sources of a theory of ornament, as expounded by Gottfried Semper. Another constant theme in Cache's writing concerns the relationship between geometry and architecture. Objectile's particular line of questioning focuses on new possibilities for joining digital design with fabrication by using digitally operated robots. Indeed, the most advanced area of digital architecture at the international level owes a great deal to his current work. Whereas architects who have replaced their draughtsmen's tables, T-squares and compasses with computers, generally speaking, have come no closer to the digital mastery of construction or manufacturing, Objectile's gamble has allowed them to design and manufacture everything simultaneously – except that in this case it is a question of designing with the infinite variability of adaptable models fully controllable geometrically. Objectile defines this as 'associative architecture': '[T]he associative aspect is in the constitution of an architectural programme, by means of software programs, in a long and seamless chain of relationships, from designing to driving the machines that manufacture the components intended for on-site assembly'.

OCEAN NORTH

Ocean North was founded in 1998 by fusing OCEAN Helsinki, OCEAN Oslo and OCEAN Cologne, three collaborating nodes of OCEAN net, which was founded in 1995. Past members include Markus Holmsten of OCEAN Helsinki, and Johan Bettum, Bonsak Schieldrop and Kim Baumann Larsen of OCEAN Oslo.

OCEAN NORTH is trans-disciplinary and multi-modal. The current members, Michael Hensel, Achim Menges and Birger Sevaldson, are an international collective of diverse disciplines and interests from urbanism to ceramics and from digital technologies to structural innovation. This pragmatic and multi-disciplinary approach – which they liken to industrial design more than architecture – employs contradictory processes of formation to design room-size installations, building design, furniture, small objects, or even websites.

World Center for Human Concerns, proposal, 2001

OCEAN NORTH's study for a World Center for Human Concerns for New York proposes a space for all peoples and cultures, whether existing or emergent. The 430 metre tall volume of the World Center provokes a sensuous image of formation, continuity and multiplicity. It remains intelligible whether one single object folds upon itself or divides, or whether two objects are entwined in conflict or fusion. The object is and becomes both one and many at the same time, suggesting the multiplicity and connectedness of human existence.

As a memorial to the drama of 11 September 2001 and a statement against all acts of violence, the volume of the World Center inscribes within itself the volume of Minoru Yamasaki's Twin Towers, which are visible as vague figures through the textured and folded skins of the new building. The World Center's spaces result from the draping and folding of the building skin around the volume of the twin towers and articulates the building volume as a set of interstitial spaces that escape a singular spatial hierarchy and homogenous relation between the built environment and its inhabitants. On the contrary, the design commences from the notion that dynamic relations between material object and human subject establish a potential space in which social, cultural, and political experience can be located.

OMA

Founded in 1975 by Rem Koolhaas, Elia and Zoe Zenghelis and Madelon Vriesendorp, OMA is a collaborative office practising architecture and urbanism.

OMA gained renown through a series of groundbreaking entries in major competitions: Parc de la Villette, Paris (1982), ZKM, Karlsruhe, Germany (1989), Tres Grande Bibliotheque and Two Libraries for Jussieu University, Paris, (1993). During these formative years OMA also realised ambitious projects, ranging from private residences to large scale urban plans: Villa dall'Ava Paris (1991), the Kunsthal Rotterdam (1992) and the House in Bordeaux (1998). In 1994, OMA completed Euralille, a 70-hectare business and civic centre in northern France comprising the European hub for high-speed trains.

Since 2001 OMA has completed numerous projects, including Casa da Musica in Porto (2005), the Prada Epicenter in Los Angeles (2004), the Seattle Public Library (2004), the Leeum Samsung Museum of Art (2004), the Netherlands Embassy in Berlin (2003), and the Prada Epicenter in New York (2001). OMA has also been engaged in several museum projects including the Whitney Museum in New York, the Los Angeles Country Museum of Art and two Guggenheim museums in Las Vegas (2001).

The work of Rem Koolhaas and OMA has won several international awards, including the Pritzker Architecture 2000, and was the subject of a retrospective exhibition held at the Museum of Modern Art, New York in 1995.

Two Libraries at Jussieu Campus, Paris, 1992
The implantation of a new library symbolises the insertion of a new core, which should at the same time revitalise the significance of Albert's original project.

However beautiful, Albert's campus is windy, cold and empty, but more important for its disfunctionality is the fact that Jussieu is a network, not a building. Its endlessness psychologically exhausts in advance any attempt to 'inhabit' it. Intended as the essence of the campus, the pedestrian parvis is experienced as a residue, a mere slice of void sandwiched between sockle and building.

To reassert its credibility, the parvis' surface is seen as pliable, a social magic carpet. It is folded to form a 'stacking' of platforms, which is then enclosed to become a building that can be read as the culmination of the Jussieu network.

These new surfaces – a vertical, intensified landscape, are then 'urbanised', almost like a city: the specific elements of the libraries are re-implanted in the new public realm like buildings in a city. Instead of a simple stacking of one floor on top of another, sections of each floor are manipulated to connect with those above and below.

CCTV Television Station and Headquarters, Beijing, China, 2002–2008
CCTV will be one among many towers in Beijing's new Central Business District, all striving to be unique – all different expressions of verticality. The tragedy of the skyscraper is that it marks a place as significant, which it then occupies and exhausts with banality. The banality is two-fold: in spite of their potential to be incubators of new cultures, programs and ways of life, most towers accommodate merely routine activity, arranged according to predictable patterns. Formally, their expressions of verticality have proven to stunt the imagination: as verticality soars, creativity crashes.

Instead of competing in the hopeless race for ultimate height – dominance of the skyline can only be achieved for a short period of time, and soon another, even taller building will emerge – the project proposes an iconographic constellation of two high-rise structures that actively engage the city space: CCTV and TVCC.

CCTV combines administration and offices, news and broadcasting, programme production and services – the entire process of TV-making – in a loop of interconnected activities. While CCTV is a secured building for staff and technology, public visitors will be admitted to the 'loop', a dedicated path circulating through the building and connecting to all elements of the program and offering spectacular views across the multiple facades towards the CBC, Beijing, and the Forbidden City.

The Television Cultural Center (TVCC) is an open, inviting structure. It accommodates visitors and guests, and will be freely accessible to the public. On the ground floor, a continuous lobby provides access to the 1500-seat theatre, a large ballroom, digital cinemas, recording studios and exhibition facilities.

Périphériques
Louis Paillard (1960) + Anne-Françoise Jumeau (1962); Emmanuelle Marin-Trottin (1967) + David Trottin (1965)

For the last eight years, Périphériques has been an evolving structure, exploring the production and spread of architecture. Currently co-ordinated by Marin+Trottin architects and Jumeau/SoA, Périphériques propose creation based on shared negotiation and ideas. Their activities are purposely multifaceted and their architectural productions divided between two firms: the Documentation for the Centre Georges Pompidou and the Maison MR for Marin+Trottin architects; the Nouveau Casino and the Maison Icône for Jumeau/SoA with L. Paillard, for example. Périphériques architectural teams also collaborate on projects such as the university building 16M for the Jussieu campus in Paris, the Centre Régional des Musiques Actuelles in Nancy, the Belvedere in Tsumari, Japan, and the Delaville café in Paris. In parallel to their involvement in architectural production, Périphériques formed an association with Franck Tallon, whose IN-EX projects is an organization for publishing and creating books. Between 2004 and 2006, they will deliver eight buildings, whose sites are breaking ground or underway: 30 experimental houses of the REX Pirotterie in Nantes; houses for the Villa Torpedo in Saint Denis; the Ecole des Beaux-Arts de Valenciennes; GO house in Thionville; the headquarters of Banlieues Bleues in Pantin; 16M for the Jussieu campus; the Media Arts Centre and Nursery School in Clamart; and the Centre Régional in Nancy.

Freaks Towers Project, proposal, 2004

For Périphériques, architects and urban planners resemble the prison characters in *Alien*, who struggle to destroy the 'monster', yet are fascinated by its evil, its strength and its adaptive abilities. They believe that in the city, the good and the evil, the beautiful and the ugly, the rich and the miserable all exist side by side. The endless succession of artefacts numbs us to the constant zapping, between disgust and fascination, at the mercy of our moods and our resources. Their tower projects stage their scenario of 'architecture-monster', the city as 'entity-monster', in that it reflects savage creative processes. Périphériques, affirming its 'rock-'n'-roll' spirit of customization, the mix of cultures and music, collage, graffiti and zapping for the critique re-reading of reality they propose, deem it urgent to experiment with alternative modes of architectural production because they open new fields without undercutting the reality they induce.

Gianni Pettena (1940)

Gianni Pettena was part of the European 'radical architecture' movement emerging in Italy, which gathered together a broad array of influential people, from Ettore Sottsass Jr. to Alessandro Mendini, from Superstudio to Archizoom. This movement questioned the identity of architecture, proclaiming it a conceptual activity that could integrate the other visual arts. Pettena appeared as an artist using the language of architecture and as an architect making use of artistic logic. His experimental work of the 1970s lies at the intersection of conceptual art and Land Art. In Pettena's approach, ideas are always tested against the scale of the human body and of the context, whether natural or urban. His work, like that of his friend James Wines, of the group SITE, continually explores the relationship between nature and architecture. His house, or 'cabin', on the island of Elba, a work in progress since 1978, is developing in nature, which is itself a kind of 'unconscious architecture'. Artist, designer, critic and respected historian of architecture, organizer of exhibitions ('Radicals, Architecture and Design 1960–1975', International Architecture Exhibition (Venice Biennale), 1996; 'Archipelago', 1999), Pettena has taught at the University of Florence since the beginning of his career. In addition to the cabin on Elba, he built the new City Hall of Canazei, Trento (1990–97).

Ice House, Minneapolis, USA, 1971–72

In Ice House I, Pettena pours water over the entire length of former administrative premises and a school. The building freezes at night, cloaking itself in a layer of translucent ice. Taking inspiration from Gordon Matta-Clark, Gianni Pettena has committed an 'act of displacement', in which architecture returns to its original material and physical state. It is now impossible to dwell anywhere; the space has been irremediably deconstructed (James Wines later saw Pettena as a precursor of deconstruction in the 1980s). In Ice House II, Pettena elaborates a structure in wood, over which he again pours water, thereby imprisoning a suburban home in a cube of ice. Ice House seeks to inoculate architecture with the immanence and transience of nature.

Walter Pichler (1936)

Following studies in graphic arts at the Vienna school of applied arts, Pichler became interested in architecture. During a trip to Paris in 1960, his discovery of prehistoric ritual sculptures strengthened the tendencies towards the archaic in his work. His encounter with Hans Hollein played a determining role in his growing interest in architecture. In 1963, this meeting resulted in an acclaimed exhibition of Hollein and Pichler's projects at the Galerie Nachst St. Stephan, Vienna. Though the exhibition lasted only a few days, it triggered radical manifestos in defence of these architectural visionaries and gave the green light to the development of the Viennese experimental architectural 'scene', from which several groups quickly emerged including Coop Himmelb(l)au and Haus-Rucker-Co. Pichler exhibited his ideas about urban architecture, hence his Compact City, which completed the early phase in the development of his architectural concepts. There followed a period of realizations of spatial installations (*Prototypen*), in which he conducted experiments with the body in a cognitive and sensory environment. In 1971, his spectacular exhibit at Museum des 20. Jahrhunderts in Vienna displayed this art of the object that conjures the aura, the cult and the senses. In parallel, he acquired a piece of property in a remote area of Austria, on the border with Hungary and near Slovenia, where he installs his life-size models. His house in St. Martin is organized concentrically around the workshop, the spatial and intellectual core, offered as a work in progress.

Compact City, 1963

The Compact City was first shown at the exhibition/manifesto 'Architektur' in 1963, mounted with Hans Hollein, at the Nachst St. Stephan gallery. The 'compact city' had become a recurring theme in architectural discourse of the period. Constructed in the shape of a tower, the city offers the possibility of infinite expansion. The 'compact city' enjoys the benefit of artificially conditioned climate, and buildings are protected from nature by solid transparent envelopes. The project expresses a radical critique of society: the intervention of architects is limited to an interior space that excludes all possibility of individual expression. This led to enthusiasm for the technique, specific to the period, which developed into the sarcastic expression of the 'prototypes' by Walter Pichler.

Ricardo Porro (1925)

Architect, sculptor, painter, furniture designer and a man of immense cultural depth, Ricardo Porro is the master builder of a vitalist architecture whose roots plunge deeply into the architecture of Gaudí, Erich Mendelsohn, Gunnar Asplund, Frank Lloyd Wright and Rudolph Steiner. Ricardo Porro grew up and studied in Havana, in the heart of the Caribbean. There in the early 1960s, he built the School of Plastic Arts and the School of Dance, which are now on UNESCO's list of world heritage sites. Already in these early buildings one finds all the elements that will define his architecture: a sense of the spatial ellipse and a sensual exuberance of form. The still-present architecture of anthropomorphism provides a symbolic image that arises from the cosmic order of the universe. The syncretism of his architecture, which links man to the world, appears as an enormous body. In 1966, Porro moved to France where he taught art history and architecture until 1992. In 1969, he built his first European work: an Art Centre to house a private collection in Liechtenstein. Porro then designed in 1972 a project for a Youth Centre in Vaduz, Liechtenstein, which looked like a drawn and quartered human body. Pushing the anthropomorphic allegory to an extreme, Ricardo Porro proposed, in a competition for a Holiday Village in Vela Luca on the island of Korcula, then in Yugoslavia (1972), to interpret each building as an element of the human body.

His association with Renaud de la Noue in 1986 multiplied the commissions Porro received in the Paris region. The buildings in their numerous housing and school programmes are more and more spectacular. Their projects evoke natural metaphors, either vegetal or animal. The plan for the Collège Elsa-Triolet in Saint-Denis (1987–90) takes the shape of a dove in flight. The Collège Colonel-Fabien in Montreuil (1990–93) relies on natural metaphors, organized round ying and yang symbols traced on the ground. The Collège for Cergy-le-Haut, Val d'Oise, comprises a hypostyle room inspired by Egyptian architecture with baroque allusions to Borromini. Believers in the dramatic effects that architecture can deliver, Porro and La Noue organized a genuine staging for the Caserne des Gardes Républicains in Vélizy (Paris; 1997–99), reinterpreting the theme of the historic scene depicted in the painting 'The Battle of San Romano' by Paolo Uccello (1456–60). Ricardo Porro is without a doubt the only contemporary architect with the capacity to make architecture of such symbolic and formal complexity, skilfully handling such a wealth of architectural, literary, pictorial and philosophical references without pastiche or citation.

Arthur Quarmby (1934)

It was in a context of international emulation focusing on plastic materials (Rudolf Doernach, Pascal Häusermann, Chanéac, Wogenscky, Ralph Erskine, Cesare Pea, Renzo Piano, Kisho Kurokawa, Kiyonori Kikutake, Kenzo Tange) that the young English architect Arthur Quarmby developed the historic junction between France and England, between Ionel Schein and Archigram. In 1961, he designed single-block cells for British Railways (Relay Room System, 1959–61). These prefabricated buildings, put up in just a few hours, were designed as electrical relay housings, required for the automation of the lines. In 1974, Quarmby published a book on research into plastics of international impact (*The Plastics Architect*, Pall Mall Press, London, 1974). In parallel, from the early 1960s onwards, he was developing inhabitable cells in plastic materials. Arthur Quarmby studied three-dimensional structures, as well as pneumatic dwellings. He then designed a 25-metre-square pneumatic cupola for the film *The Touchables* and two inflatable projects: a helium-filled cover for Wembley Stadium and a Shell service station (Baldock, Hertfordshire, UK). Influenced by the organic dwellings designed by Frederick Kiesler, Quarmby also developed plastic cell projects under a transparent climate-controlled dome.

Plydom Housing, 1962

It was without a doubt Arthur Quarmby who, in 1962, first had the idea of hooking cells on to a mast. In England, Archigram's 'plug-in' would later echo Quarmby's designs, in which cells cluster round a tower. Across the globe, hanging plastic cells began to sprout along a hollow column, a sort of vertical street: in the USA, with Paul Rudolph; in Germany, with Wolfgang Doering and Gernot Nalbach; in France, with James Guitet and, especially, Paul Maymont; in Switzerland, with Grataloup; in Japan, with Isozaki and Kurokawa, who would actually realize the first building of this type in 1971 (Nakagin Capsule Tower Building, Ginza, Tokyo).

R&Sie...
François Roche (1961), Stéphanie Lavaux (1966)

R&Sie... focuses entirely on experimentation, both theoretical and practical, at the intersection of a cross-disciplinary approach. Known for the provocative positions he took in the early 1990s, François Roche, in his manifesto *L'Ombre du caméléon (Trash mimésis)*, traced out his concept of a new kind of architecture that favours material, physical and climatic facts, in reaction to the formal and technological excess of the architecture of the 1980s that he was denouncing. Thenceforth, mapping would substitute for the traditional sketch work, the territory for the plan, the situation for the site and the stealthy for the fixed object. For Roche, 'it has nothing to do with opposing the project to its context, as if they were two distinct hypotheses, but of linking them through the very process of transformation'. Thus, he designed the project for the Route du Maïdo for the FRAC Reunion (1996) and the Memorial Museum of Soweto, Johannesburg, South Africa (1997). In 2000, R&Sie... went on to build the Maison d'Ami Barak in Sommières, Gard, a 'stealthy object' in the territory, and the Museum of Contemporary Art in Bangkok, wrapped in an electrified netting, which creates an electrostatic zone that serves to collect some of the dust of this polluted city. So, working with a critical 'hyper-localism' trending towards disorientation, François Roche and Stéphanie Lavaux refuse to design elsewhere a project to be built here, drawing from the logic of an intervention through research on the constituent elements of the territory, whence they extract their substrata and tools of production.

(Un)Plug Building, La Défense, Paris, unbuilt project, 2001

R&Sie... are fascinated with phenomena of mutation, distortion, cloning, hybridization, grafting and morphing. This 23-storey building, housing 352 'home offices', was commissioned by the electric company EDF. The façade would have generated electricity through renewable energy sources of wind and sunlight. Covered with photovoltaic cells and capillaries, the tower became a reactive membrane allowing for simultaneous energy consumption and production. The building could be plugged into the urban electrical network. R&Sie... also implemented the concept of interiors for working and living at home (home offices). These cells, which house offices, inflate in the activity phase, becoming puffy protuberances on the façade, or deflate during rest. The building thus becomes a permanent mutant, a cyborg drawing inspiration from the plugged-in cells of Archigram, finding nourishment in the work of Gilles Deleuze and science fiction.

Silverelief / B-mu, Bangkok Contemporary Art Museum, 2002

Bangkok is a very dusty and grey city but it also has a luminous quality. The pollutants in the air seem to leech out the colour of the city.

The Museum building proposal is inspired by Man Ray's famous photograph of Marcel Duchamp's 'Large Glass' entitled 'Dust Breeding'. The photograph shows a dense layer of dust obscuring the surface of the glass. The architects see Bangkok as a similar condition. The city cloaked in a dense miasma of floating particles as it goes about its business.

The building design makes this conceptual idea abundantly clear and in so doing provides Bangkok with a proposition, which is simultaneously alien and contextual. It can even be argued that the design is helping to clear the air of Bangkok by attracting dust.

The building consists of a series of interlinked blocks covered in a woolly coat. This coat is to encourage the build up of dust and urban grime around the building providing it with dynamic forever changing views out and views in.

The traditional notion of cleanliness, which has obsessed Modernist architects for over a century, is here deliberately flouted. Dirt becomes decoration and the passage of time is recorded and honoured in the constant build up of minuscule detritus.

DR_D Studio
Dagmar Richter (1955)

Dagmar Richter studied at the University of Stuttgart and then at the Royal Art Academy School of Architecture in Copenhagen, Denmark, where she obtained her diploma in 1982. In 1987, she founded Dagmar Richter Studio in Los Angeles and Berlin. Today, her firm DR_D Studio, opened in 2001, is divided between Santa Monica and Berlin. In parallel, Dagmar Richter has always taught internationally, built her own house in Santa Monica (1998) and been a finalist in many international competitions. In most of her projects, Richter uses computer processing tools to implement flexible planning – always open – of the territory, but within a world of whose instability and liquidity she is quite aware. Since the 1980s, she has substituted space with the memories of events that have composed it. This rapport with history is immediately material and tectonic, recomposing the ground in symbolic layers that the architect uses as a formal resource. 'The architect and urban planner are collectors of traces,' Richter says, 'whether historic, discovered through maps, or appearing in photographs, drawings, texts or even occurring in speech; images and words that seem, *a priori*, without any link.' DR_D Studio constantly relies on digital tools, not only for design, but also for simultaneous 3D modelling of projects.

The Wave, Aarhus, 'Gigantium' competition, Denmark, unbuilt project, 2001

This competition was for an urban and landscaped sports complex in Aarhus, Denmark. Richter's project explores a method that puts the existing topography, the landscape as cultural construct and its biological and geological processes into a relationship with sporting activities. The architecture is transformed into a complex, artificial, climatically planned landscape whose surfaces (covered with lawns, asphalt, concrete, etc.) lend themselves to sporting activities and different games, under the effects of snow or sunshine. Everything dissolves into the topography of sleek and undulating surfaces.

Michele Saee (1956)

Born in Tehran, Michele Saee studied at the Florence School of Architecture. In 1985, he founded his own firm, Building Inc., in Los Angeles. His architecture, always unstable and in an almost unfinished state, looks like an assemblage of floating shapes, successive envelopes of a composite body in motion. Genuinely sculptural surfaces interacting with light, his houses (Artist Studio, Golzari House, Meivsahna House), free of any formal typology, are ordered according to overlapping and interlocking folds, fault lines and fractures. Michele Saee also uses his houses to undertake a critique of California's urban spaces, close to a 'non-city' in an intermediate stage. An experienced builder, he has constructed numerous public spaces in the USA (Trattoria Angeli, Los Angeles, 1987; Ecru Store, 1988; Design Express, 1989; Angeli Mare, Los Angeles, 1989–90), as well as in Italy (International Centre for Comparative Cultural Studies, Sardinia, 1999–2003) and recently in Paris, France (Drugstore Publicis, Champs-Elysées, 2003; Café Nescafé, 2002). The façade of the Drugstore Publicis, which houses a restaurant, cinema, bookstore and shops, deploys a spectacular glass envelope covering all sides, opposite the Arc de Triomphe. His intervention breathes a surprising new dynamism into one of the most famous classical architectural structures in the world. Here, as in most of his projects and buildings, Michele Saee moulds light materials into broadly open and available spaces.

Meivsahna House, Los Angeles, California, unbuilt project, 1991

The Meivsahna House looks like a vessel grounded on its side and fractured into two parts down a central line. The use of the elements strives to maintain continuity. Only changes in materials, differences in ceiling height and sloping floors mark the passage from one space to another. Michele Saee allows the general skeleton of the building to show through, evoking the superimpositions of patterns used in haute couture. Geometric forms and biometric curves overlap. The model is presented as a stacking of thin forms whose volumes are organized into a thoracic cavity; the envelope becomes a flexible and open carapace; the interior, a living organism feeding on the exterior.

Ionel Schein (1927)

Architect, urban planner and architectural historian, Bucharest-born Ionel Schein is one of architecture's major figures. After an association with Claude Parent, in 1955, Ionel Schein began experimenting with new material. For him, architects, engineers and industrialists must work together. In 1956, he invented the very first plastic house, a feat blessed with a fertile architectural posterity, including House of the Future by Alison and Peter Smithson in 1956 in London and Monsanto House by Dietz, Heger, McGarry, Hamilton and Goody in 1957 in the USA. That same year in Belgium, Jacques Baudon and François Jamagne developed a farm almost entirely made of plastic. From 1958, Pascal Häusermann was studying houses in the shape of plastic eggs (Domobiles). In 1960, Chanéac created the prototype for a multipurpose cell in plastic. In 1961, Arthur Quarmby, working in England, built shelters and railway electrical relay housings in single plastic blocks. In 1961, at the Paris Home Furnishings Fair, André Wogenscky presented his tower, a new prototype for a plastic house. In 1962, Russian architects in Leningrad designed a plastic house. The futuristic work of Ionel Schein was also a point of departure for new trends that would revolutionize architecture, involving notions of mobility, assembly and do-it-yourself construction.

Plastic-Made House, prototype, Paris, 1956

In April 1955, Ionel Schein, then aged 29, working in collaboration with Y. Magnant (engineer) and R.A. Coulon (architect), designed the first 'all-plastic' house. In February 1956, the full-scale model was shown at the Paris Home Furnishings Fair. Financing had come from Charbonnages de France and Houillères du Nord, encouraged by the possible leverage the house represented for promoting new applications of plastic materials extracted from coal. Fourteen varieties of plastic were utilized. Even all the furnishings were in plastic. Schein advocated the plastic materials for three main reasons: quality of implementation, light weight and speed of production. The house in plastic attracted an extraordinary amount of attention and received over 200,000 visitors. For Ionel Schein, architecture in plastic is the architecture of life. The house settles into an organic rhythm of growth with its snail plan. This simple, naturally occurring form affords a remarkably functional interior organization. Nature grows, like the family.

Mobile Cabin Hotel, prototype, Paris, 1956

In October 1956, Schein, pursuing his research with the same team, imagined a fully equipped and mobile hotel room, shaped like a single shell, upright and moulded in laminated plastic materials and fibreglass. This mobile cabin hotel was displayed in its plaster prototype form in Paris. The cabins allowed for rapid transport and installation on all types of terrain and became the very first autonomous dwelling units that could be transported by lorry. Reyner Banham, the Pop Art critic and member of Archigram in England, published the design in 1961 in a famous article entitled 'Stocktaking' that appeared in *Architectural Review*. Industrial production of these housing units in plastic should, in Schein's view, free people from their 'inscription'. After Archigram, Schein's influence spread to the

Metabolists. In 1956, Kurokawa visited Schein's offices and learnt of the project for making plastic hotel cabins. In 1970, Kurokawa presented his dwelling-capsule at the World Fair in Osaka, proclaiming, 'The capsule is cyborg architecture.' A new space composed of modularity, proliferation and clustering – agglomeration – of cells settled into place.

Alison & Peter Smithson
(1928-1993), (1923-2003)

In 1952 the Smithsons won the competition for the now well-known Hunstanton School. Their interest in the white and clean lines of pre-war international Modernism was augmented and redirected by stringent post-war cost considerations and they became influential in creating the 'Brutalist' style.

In 1956 they contributed to the seminal 'This is Tomorrow' exhibition at the Whitechapel Art Gallery in London. Also in the same year they created the prototype 'House of the Future' for the Daily Mail Ideal Home Exhibition. In 1959 they were commissioned for the Economist Building in London. In the late 60s and 70s they created the social housing of Robin Hood Gardens, Tower Hamlets. They continued to practise until their deaths and a collected anthology of their work, 'the Charged Void' was published in 2002.

House of the Future, Ideal Home Exhibition, Olympia, London, 1956

After the end of the Second World War, architects had a wealth of new materials and manufacturing techniques with which to experiment. The House of the Future was a prototype of a new way of creating dwellings. It was prefabricated and it was moulded plastic. Domestic appliances were supposed to be 'built in', part of the sensual undulations of the walls. The house had a double-curved roof and was designed to facilitate sunlight penetration and rain water run-off. The roof was also reflective to avoid undue passive solar-heat gain.

The house was a harbinger for much of what was to follow in the 'Megastructural' years of the 60s. All the iconic pods, capsules and gasket housing designs of the avant-garde of this later period owe more than a little to the Smithsons' House of the Future.

Graham Stevens (1944)

As an exercise in systematic design methods at Sheffield University in 1965, Stevens designed a pneumatic condiment set using balloons. The response of fellow students made him realize the potential for pneumatic environments. Spacefield (1966) integrated light (colour and electromagnetic field), sound, smell, taste, tactile and kinaesthetic experience in an air structure. Over the following ten years, he developed the energy and participatory aspects of pneumatic structures, inventing Waterbed, Walking on Water, Bean Bag, Bouncy Castle (all 1966) and Desert Cloud (1972–74), which condensed atmospheric water in desert climates. Films he made of these structures in the United Kingdom and Kuwait led to invitations for his architectural practice to work in all climate zones; as a result he designed a Hajj walkway shade structure in Saudi Arabia (1981), a rainforest in Egypt (1984), a renewable energy programme in Uganda (1986) and ecotourism villages or towns in Spain (1977), Brunei (1991), Tanzania (1993) and Sinai (1994). Since 1991 he has been studying legal barriers to implementing environmental projects and solutions to global warming, stemming from the power imbalance between artists and lawyers in the UK. Several of his works are patented, particularly applications of general principles developed in art and in the architectural solutions of what he terms an 'informed' architecture.

Desert Cloud, installation, 1972–74

This pneumatic structure has been developed from the earlier work Atmospheric Raft (1969), expressing the energy exchanges in the atmosphere and the possibility of transforming the atmospheric energy of the sun, wind, rain and electricity for architecture and the environment. ICI chemicals donated the Melinex® high-clarity polyester film and the Arts Council of Great Britain awarded a grant to film the structure operating in the Arabian desert. The film not only documents the first solar flight but also explores future applications of the scientific principles of optically selective membranes in agriculture, architecture, transport and water production in deserts.

Superstudio (1966–82)
Adolfo Natalini (1941), Cristiano Toraldo di Francia (1941), Roberto Magris (1935), Piero Frassinelli (1939), Alessandro Magris (1941), Alessandro Poli (1941)

Florence, Italy, the very heart of 'radical architecture' (as described by the art critic Germano Celant), played host to, among others, the groups Archizoom, Superstudio and UFO, who proclaimed their iconoclastic approach, a conceptual practice associating architecture with the other arts. Projects, furniture prototypes and texts from Superstudio betrayed the influence of 'Anglo-Saxon' Pop culture, which they interpreted with an ideological twist, with provocative, critical and ironic accents. Between 1971 and 1973, the group worked in the field of 'operative criticism', making films popularizing utopian projects. They were seeking the road to a philosophical and anthropological re-foundation for architecture. Their projects were exhibited in 1972 at the show 'Italy: The New Domestic Landscape' at the MoMA in New York. Histograms of Architecture (1969) and Continuous Monument (1971) were the group's two most notable projects. In them, architecture became a system of abstract conception of 'neutral and available entities'. Continuous Monument represents a proposal for an 'architectural model for total urbanization'. Architecture utilizes a radical tool for criticism, through an uninterrupted monumental structure, intended as a course for traversing the planet. Superstudio participated in the XVth and XVIth Milan Triennales; in 1973, they figured among the founders of Global Tools, a system of workshops for developing collective creativity.

Histograms of Architecture, 1969–2001

The Histograms of Architecture, or The Tombs of the Architects, are a catalogue of three-dimensional isotropic diagrams with homogeneous surfaces. The Histograms are a theoretical proposition, which can be transferred to any scale, whether domestic, architectural or urban, exploring different semantics, yet all the while remaining themselves. They are 'seeking an inalterable image', an immutable representation of architecture. The outcome of a general reductive process, they are the 'projection of Platonic abstractions'. The radical nature of Superstudio's Histograms, the elements of a conceptual architecture, achieves the disappearance of the notion of 'quality' in architecture. Their framework invades all – territory, furnishings, architecture and city, in a 'thorough review of the typologies of classicism'. Architecture is nothing more than a mental diagram, a grid without beginning or end.

Pierre Székely (1923–2001)

Born in Hungary, Pierre Székely, 'sculptor architect', settled in France in 1946, where he was making his mark by the early 1950s as a pioneer in the integration of sculpture with architecture. Székely dedicated himself to the 'synthesis of the plastic arts through architecture', as Michel Ragon wrote. His approach fits into the context of the new sensitivity regarding space that developed in the aftermath of the war; to this sensitivity one can also relate the sculptures of Jean Dubuffet, the homes of Etienne-Martin, the sculpture-dwellings of André Bloc, the sculptures and urban projects of Marino di Teana and the architecture of Jacques Couëlle. In 1952–53, Székely drew up plans for the house called Le Bateau Ivre in Saint-Marcellin (Isère). It was built in 1956 and is one of the first examples of an effective fusion of the artistic and architectural approaches. In 1957, he realized the first 'practicable' sculpture for the children of Petit-Clamart outside Paris, with the architect Robert Auzelle. In 1962, in collaboration with the architect François Bride, he elaborated the project of a Cité Spirituelle for the town of Rheims, but it was never built. In 1964, he imagined a flying sculpture for the floating island belonging to the architect Paul Maymont.

In 1965, Székely joined the GIAP (Groupe International d'Architecture Prospective, futurist architects), founded by the critic Michel Ragon, which brought together the most forward-looking artists and architects of the day. That same year, he built the Village of Culture and Leisure in Beg-Meil, Brittany, in partnership with the architect Henri Mouette. In 1965, he exhibited his utopian project for the Aerial City, an orbiting satellite, at the Congress of the International Union of Architects in Paris. In 1966, he completed construction on one of the most significant works of architecture-sculpture, the Eglise du Carmel de Saint-Saulve, outside Valenciennes, designed in collaboration with the architect Claude Guislain. In 1973 and 1974, he built two house-sculptures, working again with the architect Henri Mouette. They used the technique of sprayed concrete, which allowed them to develop curved shapes that looked as if they had been modelled by a sculptor. For these projects, as for his first house for the Gelas, Székely invited his clients to participate in the creative development processes of their house. A tireless creator, Székely once declared, 'What amuses me is building utopia in the present'.

Kenzo Tange (1913–2005)

Born in Osaka, Kenzo Tange studied under Kunio Maekawa, a student of Le Corbusier. He was the one of the first Japanese architects to gain worldwide recognition and work internationally, and in Japan he enjoys a status at the pinnacle of architecture. Well-known works include the Hiroshima Peace Centre, The New Tokyo City Hall Complex, National Gymnasiums for the Tokyo Olympics, Master Plan for Expo '70, Sogetsu Hall and Office, Tokyo Metropolitan Government Office and the Fuji Television Headquarters Building. He has also trained many of the leading architects in Japan today, including Yukio Otani, Takashi Asada, Tanero Oki, Fumihiko Maki, Koji Kamiya, Arata Isozaki, Kisho Kurokawa and Yoshio Taniguchi. He gained international renown when he won the first prize in the Hiroshima Peace Memorial Urban Planning Competition in 1949, and presented his plans for Hiroshima to the International Congress of Modern Architecture (CIAM) in 1951. His work has a characteristic clarity of structure permeating the project from overall layout to design of individual buildings.

In 1960, his plan for rebuilding Tokyo, A Plan for Tokyo 1960 – Towards a Structural Reorganization, proposed the extension of Tokyo's infrastructure into the centre of Tokyo Bay, calling this a *civic axis*. The plan went as far as providing practical designs, following his approach of considering how individual functions would be linked together and linked in with the overall design.

Both his Plan for Tokyo and his Community Plan for 25,000 People (1960), which immediately preceded it, clearly demonstrated an archetype of megastructure-style urban planning, and are considered to have provided the inspiration for the young architects, particularly those working in Tange's firm, to start the Metabolism movement. Later, his Master Plan for Expo '70, and his Omatsuri Hiroba (Festival Plaza) cemented his position as the architect representing Japan to the outside world.

The involvement of Tange's staff such as Arata Isozaki and Kisho Kurokawa at the time not only was important for the practical realization of these proposals but also gave a strong boost to their growth and professional development. In 1986, when Tokyo was planning to move its City Hall to Shinjuku, Tange won the competition and was contracted to design the New Tokyo Metropolitan Government Office. He also worked on the Fuji Television Headquarters Building, the symbol of the urban development project for Tokyo Bay. Tange embodies the post-war growth that made Japan an economic superpower and he has had a substantial and significant effect on the history of architecture worldwide.

Yamanashi Press and Broadcasting Centre, Kofu 1961–66
This is a building with classical megastructure-like elements. The Centre provides facilities for a media group, including newspapers, broadcasting and printing company operations. The common infrastructure is concentrated in a number of 'pipes' – 5-metre-diameter cylinders – that run vertically through the building. The pipes incorporate basic infrastructure functions such as stairs, elevators, air-conditioning facilities and electrical wiring. The design permits floor surfaces to be widened, enabling flexible growth. The media group that owns the building has in fact extended it several times, and the additions are not obvious from the outside. The history of Metabolism shows that in most cases Metabolist buildings have not grown or been extended at all, which is a negation of the 'metabolic' concept. The Yamanashi Press and Broadcasting Centre is a happy exception to that record. The design and materials have given the building a menacing, brutal air. Tange's design has the visually oppressive feel of a megastructure, and is one of the most 'symbolic' of his works.

Bernard Tschumi (1944)
A native of Switzerland, Bernard Tschumi studied at the Zurich Polytechnic Institute. Initially focused on teaching at the Architectural Association in London (1970–79) and the Institute for Architecture and Urban Studies in New York (1976), he currently dedicates his time to advancing architectural theory and drawing up 'manifestos'. These include *Manhattan Transcripts* and *Screenplays* (1976–81),

which provided the inspiration for a first series of experimental and ephemeral constructions, called Folies and built in London, New York and the Netherlands, notably La Case Vide (1986), Cinégramme Folie and Parc de la Villette (1987). Many of his essays, written between 1975 and 1991, have been assembled in the work *Architecture and Disjunction*. Having ceased teaching in 1983, he swiftly achieved a standing as a leading representative of deconstruction with his creation of one of the most prestigious commissions of the 1980s, the redevelopment of the former Paris abattoirs into the Parc de la Villette. Associated with the 1988 exposition 'Deconstructivist Architecture' in New York, he developed his reflection, which was not linked to form or the 'inscription' of architecture, but focused rather on space, movement and the event. Bernard Tschumi then received other important commissions, such as the Pavilion of the Video in Groningen, Netherlands (1990), the Studio National des Arts Contemporains in Tourcoing, France (1991–97), the Lerner Hall at Columbia University in New York (1994–99), the Ecole d'Architecture in Marne-la-Vallée, France (1994–99) and the Zénith theatre in Rouen (1998–2001). Dean from 1988 to 2003 of the Graduate School of Architecture, Planning and Preservation at Columbia University, he has received many prizes in his career.

Parc de la Villette, Paris, built 1983–92

The programme for Parc de la Villette envisaged gathering numerous cultural, pedagogic, sporting and leisure activities on a single site of 55 hectares. Tschumi decided to use a process of dissemination by distributing the elements of the programme across the entire site. Located at the city's edge, a place for meeting, exchange and cultural blending, the Parc de la Villette had to provide solutions for three kinds of requirements: the officially defined activities, circulation and areas for sports and games. Tschumi's answer included three systems, superimposed: the *points* materialized by the Folies, red metallic constructions, dispersed across the framework; the *lines*, curving or straight, indicating paths of circulation; and the *surfaces*, defined by broad green spaces for playing fields. These systems overlap and criss-cross each other within a vast framework, inviting the stroller to switch from one usage to another. The design for the park and its events finds its origin in the *Manhattan Transcripts* and the *Screenplays*, notations influenced by post-structuralist texts and diverse cinematographic editing techniques. The red pavilions also pay homage to Melnikov and Russian constructivism. For Bernard Tschumi, architecture is not an autonomous discipline defined in terms of form or style, but rather a combination of heterogeneous, even incompatible fragments.

UN Studio
Ben van Berkel (1956), Caroline Bos (1959)

A native of Utrecht, Ben van Berkel studied at the Architectural Association in London under the direction of Rem Koolhaas and Zaha Hadid. After working with Santiago Calatrava, he opened his own firm in 1988 in Amsterdam with his associate Caroline Bos, an art historian. In 1998, they changed the name of their firm to UN Studio (United Net Studio). In their manifesto, *Move* (1999), Van Berkel and Bos develop the roles they assign to the architect of today: engagement in the practices of networks, a deeply thought-out approach to development of the plan, the will to invent, commitment in favour of the public space and speed. Deeply rooted in networked thinking and oriented towards interdisciplinary collaboration, their practice pulls together all the aspects of a project – technological, conceptual and constructive – through close collaboration with teams of urban planners, industrialists, graphic artists, economists, administrators, designers and photographers, in which each participates on an equal footing. UN Studio's activity has resulted in a wide variety of projects, from small to large, mainly built in the Netherlands, but also in Austria: bridges, tunnels (Erasmus Bridge, Rotterdam, 1995–98), office buildings (Spido Company, Rotterdam, 1994–2002), a power station in Austria (REMU station, 1992–93), public buildings (Musical Theatre, Graz, Austria, not built, 1998–2002; Valkhof Museum, Nijmegen, 1995–99), houses (Möbius House, 1993–98; Villa Wilbrink, 1993), collective housing in Nijmegen and Arnhem (1994–96) and urban projects (plans for the centres of Arnhem, Utrecht and Emmen). In 2002, they won the competition for the New Museum of Mercedes-Benz in Stuttgart (delivery 2006), a fluid and continuous space in the form of a clover leaf, which integrates the most advanced technological components.

Möbius House, Het Gooi, Netherlands, built 1993–98

Completely designed with computers, the house takes a mathematical paradox as its starting point: the Möbius strip, a surface with only a single edge and a single side and formed by twisting a strip of paper. 'The idea for the Möbius House project began with a diagram of two intersecting lines, which crystallized our theories on the two users of the house, husband and wife, who would eventually live and work in this home.' So, at the project's inception there was a diagram, worked out in such a way as to generate a spatial organization developing temporality in the distribution of the programme's elements. The house, with a surface area of 550m2, resembles an unfolding strip without beginning or end, distributing the various spaces in an unbroken sequence, leading from day into night and from work to rest with possible meeting places along the way. Concrete combines with the transparency of the glass walls to accentuate fluidity and the interpenetration of the spaces. The interior spaces dissolve into the landscape of the 2-hectare site.

Eisaku Ushida (1954) & Kathryn Findlay (1953)

Findlay is an Alumni of the Architectural Association, another product of the AA's halcyon days (late 70s and 80s.) She was strongly influenced by Ranulph Glanville, but perhaps more steered in terms of design and form by Christine Hawley, Leon van Schaik and Peter Cook. After graduation she developed a fascination for all things Japanese, and worked in Arata Isozaki's office where she met her future husband, Eisaku Ushida. Their separation prompted her return to London.

Ushida and Findlay's main tactic, of attempting to disentangle the country-city dichotomy, that of the natural and artificial, the husbanded and self-sown, the sleek and the rough, is the known as their notion of material 'flow'. Materials seem to flow over between and through their work, whether man-made or biological. This quality creates an 'endless' aesthetic. As well as the lack of differentiation between floor and wall, inside and outside are seldom simply defined, the landscape and its myriad drivers and devices are fully integrated with the buildings.

Truss Wall House, built, 1990–93 and Soft and Hairy Houses, built, 1992–93

These two projects illustrate the beginning of Ushida & Findlay's preoccupations with organic, wrapped around form, their penchant for the 'berming' of landscape over parts of their buildings, and their ability to transcend the usual protocols of roof, wall and floor. These works, done when Kathryn Findlay was still calling

Japan 'home' had a wide resonance and impact across the world. Anyone who really cared about the development of architecture watched the flowering of these unusual gems with delight.

Their space manifests itself as the surprising aesthetic and pragmatic juxtapositions that occur almost by accident. This approach of combining what at first might be seen as incompatible is plainly seen in these houses, built in Japan. Their strange, otherworldly quality would not be conspicuous on the set of Roger Vadim's 1968 film Barbarella and they oddly anticipate many of the stylistic predilections of some of today's new young architects.

Makoto Sei Watanabe (1952)

Born in Kanagawa Prefecture, Japan, Makoto Sei Watanabe graduated from the Yokohama National University in 1976, then joined Arata Isozaki & Associates in 1979. Five years later, he went independent, setting up his own architecture and design firm. Watanabe has received large numbers of awards and has lectured at several universities. His architecture emerges from direct interaction with cities, and for him, a guided city is actually a continuously evolving event. Watanabe exploits the positive energy of chaos and of disorder in complex buildings to design a fluid dynamic like that seen in his Aoyama Technical College (1988–90), a machine created with a chaotic assembly of parts.

For Watanabe, gravity is the most important constraint on architecture. Through experimental housing projects such as his Jellyfish Series (1990–97), he has attempted to liberate the architecture from all gravitational effects to emphasize the fluctuating nature of space. These experiments have borne fruit in Mura-no Terrace (1995), a community facility for Sakauchi Village, in which a magnificently cantilevered terrace deck stretches out into a valley with a river some 12 metres below. Another embodiment of the experiments is K-Museum (1996), a facility for explaining and demonstrating the underground infrastructure in Tokyo's waterfront zone. K-Museum is a development of the Jellyfish 2 experiment, and is partly suspended in mid-air. The complexity of its form brings together minimalist volumes with high-tech materials, contrasting with the organic form of a transparent cell like a suction bulb grafted on to the structure.

How state-of-the-art technology can be integrated with the urban or natural landscape is a constant preoccupation for Watanabe. Iidabashi Subway Station, Tokyo – a multiple award-winner – has structures interlaced into a computer-designed 3D network above the stairs, escalators and platforms. His most recent projects utilize this interaction between architecture and computer to explore all the possibilities of non-standard architecture.

Jellyfish Series 1990–97

The Jellyfish Series was an experiment with light, water and gravity, exploring balance and instability, transparency and opacity. The series consists of clusters of housing with transparent modules or grafted cells, the spaces being filled with fluid to disperse light. The modules take the form of scales that measure the weight of spaces or measure the total amount of light, giving movement to the buildings.

James Wines & SITE
James Wines (1932)

James Wines is an artist, architect and architectural theorist (*De-Architecture*, 1987). For him, architecture is public art, and 'the responsibility of architecture – like any "public" art – is to communicate'. Architecture is experienced in its fluctuating, indeterminate dimension, subject to the vagaries of chance. Since the late 1960s, James Wines worked on this issue of architecture within its surrounding space, opening the way to integration of art, technology and nature. From the 1970s, SITE earned international attention with works such as Indeterminate Façade, Houston (1975) or the Inside/Outside Building, Milwaukee (1984), with unfinished brick façades, for the BEST department stores. In 1981, the Highrise of Homes project implemented a radically innovative design for the integration of nature and architecture, with buildings composed of individual houses with a garden. James Wines is based in New York and his approach integrates social, psychological and ecological aspects of the environment. He built several projects for public spaces that incorporate these elements, notably a park in a shopping centre in Toyama, Japan. His current projects include a sculpture garden and a pavilion for the Rossini Foundation in Briosco, Italy. Wines is author of more than 150 architectural projects and his drawings and models have been exhibited in over 100 museums and galleries throughout the world. James Wines advocates a form of 'environmental thinking', based on an approach to architecture and design that is both more socially aware and more responsible vis-à-vis the context and the environment.

BEST Indeterminate Façade, Houston, Texas, built 1975

Indeterminate Façade seems suspended between construction and demolition. A cascade of bricks tumbles from the wall, invading the public space and the street. Passers-by find themselves involved in direct confrontation with the building: is the building a ruin or merely under construction? In the BEST stores, the 'building changes very little physically, but a great deal psychologically', Wines remarks. This asserted ambiguity also evokes the contemporaneous theories of Robert Venturi, from *Complexity and Contradiction in Architecture* (1966) to *Learning from Las Vegas* (1977), as well as the notion of 'decorated shed', whose façade is detached from the rest of the architecture, in the manner of a BEST store. Wines calls upon the irrational and the equivocal to shake up our approach to architecture.

Lebbeus Woods (1940-)

Lebbeus Woods trained as an architect and engineer and has worked for Eero Saarinen & Associates and in private practice. In 1976 he turned to theory and experimental projects and co-founded the NY based Research Institute for Experimental Architecture (RIEA). He has been a Visiting Professor at Harvard, Columbia and the Cooper Union. He has published numerous books, including Origins, Anarchitecture: Architecture is a Political Act, and Radical Reconstruction. Woods is an accomplished draughtsman and his architecture directly questions the form/function dialectic in architecture, the politics of reconstruction after the ravages of war and the provision of the appropriate types of architecture for areas of natural disaster. His early work dealt with cybernetic metaphysics to posit new ways of living.

High Houses, Sarajevo, unbuilt, 1994–ongoing

The High Houses are part of a series of projects that Lebbeus Woods created after being deeply affected by the destruction of the Balkan Wars in the early 1990s. Contemporary redevelopment wisdom was to knock down partly destroyed buildings and replace them with more economically viable commercial structures. Woods sees this as architectural imperialism. A city, like a human being, has memories, and these memories, even the unpleasant ones, make it what it is.

So Woods patched up the city, using the analogies of 'scabs' and 'scars' and presiding over these trauma healing interventions are his High Houses that perch on tensioned stilts over the city. He designed houses that are to be inhabited but are studiously unprescriptive in their spaces. The microcosm of human liberty must be visible in the way we choose to live.

Overleaf. NOX (Lars Spuybroek)
ParisBRAIN
2001

OMA
Partners in Charge: Ole Scheeren & Rem Koolhaas
CCTV Television Station and Headquarters
Beijing, China, 2002 (completion 2008)

acknowledgements

exhibition lenders

All loans are from Collection Fondation Regional d'Art
Contemporain du Centre (FRAC Centre), Orléans, unless
as follows:

Will Alsop
Nigel Coates
dECOi (Mark Goulthorpe)
Delft University of Technology
Diller + Scofidio
EZCT Architecture & Design Research
Kathryn Findlay
Foreign Office Architects (FOA)
Future Systems
Hans Hollein
Jakob & MacFarlane
Kiyonori Kikutake
Kol/Mac Studio
Rem Koolhaas / OMA
MVRDV
Netherlands Architecture Institute (NAi)
NOX (Lars Spuybroek)
OCEAN NORTH
Collection of CNAC/MNAM, Centre Georges Pompidou
Smithson Family Collection
Tange Associates
UN Studio (Ben van Berkel & Caroline Bos)
Eisaku Ushida
Lebbeus Woods

The exhibition has been curated by Jane Alison, Curator,
Barbican Art Gallery in collaboration with Marie-Ange
Brayer, Director of FRAC Centre, Orlèans and assisted by
Louise Vaughan, Assistant Curator and Clementine
Hampshire, Exhibition Assistant.

Barbican Art Gallery is especially indebted to Lucas Dietrich
and Jamie Camplin at Thames & Hudson for enabling and
supporting the publication of this important book. It has
been thoughtfully designed by Peter Dawson at Grade
Design Consultants. We are grateful to Marie-Ange Brayer,
Frédéric Migayrou, Claude Parent and Paul Virilio, and
Fumio Nanjo for granting the rights to reproduce their texts.

Farshid Moussavi of Foreign Office Architects, together
with Brett Steele, Director of the Architectural Association;
Professor Jonathan Hill of The Bartlett School of Architecture;
Neil Spiller, Professor of Architecture & Digital Theory,
The Bartlett School of Architecture; and Aaron Betsky,
Director of the Netherlands Architecture Institute have all
generously shared ideas and insights with Jane Alison,
as the project has developed.

First published in paperback in the United Kingdom in 2007 by Thames & Hudson Ltd, 181A High Holborn, London WC1V 7QX

www.thamesandhudson.com

Published on the occasion of the exhibition 'Future City: Experiment and Utopia in Architecture', curated by Jane Alison, Barbican Art Gallery, in collaboration with Marie-Ange Brayer, Director, FRAC Centre, Orléans.

British Library Cataloguing-in-Publication Data.

A catalogue record for this book is available from the British Library.

ISBN-13: 978-0-500-28651-7
ISBN-10: 0-500-28651-5

Printed and bound in Spain by Grafos S.A.

Design Grade Design Consultants, London

Editors Jane Alison, Melissa Jones, Neil Spiller and Louise Vaughan

Introductory section texts Jane Alison, Marie-Ange Brayer, Frédéric Migayrou and Neil Spiller in collaboration with Melissa Jones

Architect biographies and project overviews
Sophie Bellé, Matthias Boeckl, Marie-Ange Brayer, Pierre Chabard, Bénédicte Chaljub, Céline Delattre, Marie-Helene Fabre, Hughes Fontenas, Christel Frapier, Christian Girard, Nadine Labedade, Christelle Lecoeur, Zeynep Mennan, Frédéric Migayrou, Philippe Morel, Fumio Nanjo (Arata Isozaki, Kiyonori Kikutake, Kisho Kurokawa, Kenzo Tange and Makoto Sei Watanabe), Frédéric Nantois, Claire Perraton, Gaia Pettena, Stéphanie Peyrissac, Pierre Roche, Richard Scoffier, Béatrice Simonot, Camille de Singly, Neil Spiller (Will Alsop, Nigel Coates, Diller+Scofidio, EZCT, Foreign Office Architects, Jakob & MacFarlane, Rem Koolhaas, MVRDV, Ocean North, OMA, R&Sie..., Alison and Peter Smithson, Eisaku Ushida & Kathryn Findlay, Lebbeus Woods), Jaqueline Stanic (Hans Hollein, Graham Stevens).

This book reprints selected texts and images originally published in Archilab's Urban Experiments: Radical Architecture, Art and the City. Edited by Marie-Ange Brayer, Frédéric Migayrou and Fumio Nanjo. Published in Japan in Japanese by Heibonsha and in English by Thames & Hudson Ltd, London.

Translations from French: Simon Pleasance, Gammon Sharpley, Fronza Woods.
Translations from Japanese: Alfred Birnbaum.

The texts by Claude Parent and Paul Virilio on pp 119–124 are translated from the magazine Architecture Principe 1966, nos 1,2,3,6 (re-edited de l'Imprimeur, Paris 1966)